Seduction Without Tears

Seduction
Without Tears

A Man's Roadmap to Dating Success

MICK C. ALEXANDER

DISCLAIMER

When you purchase or read this guide, you're stepping into an exciting realm of exploration and personal growth. However, while the content in this book is intended for informational purposes, it should not be regarded as an absolute truth.

The diverse world of human interactions means there's no one-size-fits-all approach and you can adapt the information as you see fit. Nevertheless, information can be interpreted and understood in many different ways, and I do not assume responsibility for any misinterpretation or alternate use of the content.

Here, I've shared my perspective on the subject, but please remember that you're responsible for your own choices and actions. The possibilities are vast, and the outcomes you achieve are a reflection of your unique path.

CONTENTS

TERMINOLOGY

In this guide, I'll use the terms "women," "ladies," or "girls" interchangeably to refer to the female gender. It's important to note that these terms are not tied to any specific age group. So, when you come across the word "woman" or "lady" in a sentence, it doesn't necessarily imply a mature woman. Similarly, when I use the term "girl," it doesn't imply teenagers or college-aged individuals. The insights within this book are adaptable to individuals of any age who may pique your interest.

INTRODUCTION

Welcome aboard! You're about to embark on a journey into the captivating world of dating, guided by this comprehensive playbook. But let's get one thing straight from the get-go – I'm not here to sell you the mythical elixir of seduction. There's no universal remote control in the realm of human connections, especially when it comes to the enigmatic world of women. They're as wonderfully diverse as a palette of colors, and just like a captivating novel, each page holds a new surprise. However, I've noticed something fascinating: beneath that beautiful kaleidoscope of personalities, they do have some common threads in their preferences for men.

Before we start, remember this isn't a magical spell book promising instant success. It's a resource born from years of mingling with a diverse cast of incredible women. Consider this guide your map, compass, and maybe a few playful nudges in the right direction.

But here's the fun part – there's no need to follow a rigid script. I'm not here to turn you into a smooth-talking robot. Think of this book as a toolshed filled with gadgets, each waiting for your creative touch. While I'll share useful strategies, it's your unique personality that'll breathe life into them.

So, remember, this isn't the gospel of seduction; it's more like a lively conversation with a friend who's been around the block. By the time you reach the end, you'll have the keys to unlock not just your potential but also the hearts of the amazing women you'll meet.

To get the most from this guide, I encourage you not to skip ahead. Follow the path sequentially, savoring every step. Exercise patience and approach each section with confidence. By doing so, you'll unlock the keys to a world where enriching connections with women become an enjoyable and fulfilling part of your life.

You'll soon discover the secret sauce to becoming utterly irresistible. We're talking about how to initiate conversations, communicate effectively, flirt with confidence, and create meaningful connections with women you've never met before. Trust me, it's like a magic trick without the rabbit.

As you delve into the dating world, you'll encounter a variety of situations. That's why it's crucial to think of this guide as your dating Swiss Army knife. Adapt these techniques to your unique personality, like customizing your favorite pizza. What's a win for me might be a hilarious failure for you, so always keep this in mind.

You'll also gain insights into real-life situations and the mysteries of dating apps. But beware, in the grand play of dating, there's always the chance of a curveball. Sometimes, it's like trying to juggle flaming torches while riding a unicycle. Some connections may fizzle out like a soda left open too long. It happens, and it's not always within your control. Don't let it rain on your parade.

So, remember, every interaction is a learning experience, an opportunity for growth and learning on your path to building successful relationships. Embrace the journey, soak in every experience, and always keep that smile on your face as you navigate the quirky and fascinating world of seduction!

How and Why this Book was Written

Well, just to be crystal clear, this isn't one of those academic monstrosities with references to studies that will put you to sleep. I'm not here to dazzle you with scientific proof but to dish out some advice based on my journey and the wisdom I've learned from observing others.

A wise lady once told me that no woman is governed by reason when she's in love, and I can't argue with that. In fact, all those pickup tactics and dating manuals are built on one solid foundation – the belief that women aren't falling for men because of some grand, rational theory. Nope, it's all about feelings. It's like a heart rollercoaster, and if she's not catching that thrill, no amount of PowerPoint presentations can change her mind. And you know what? My escapades in the love department have confirmed this a gazillion times. That's why, in this guide, we'll explore all the elements known to stir those essential emotions in a woman, igniting her genuine desire for you.

Now, if you happen to have some experience with women or this isn't your first rodeo with dating advice, you might be familiar with some of the basics covered within these pages. But my goal is to show you that winning a woman's affection doesn't require any elaborate pickup philosophy, complex formulas, NLP tricks, mind games, or shady tactics. It's all about cultivating a magnetic personality and finding that special connection. In this book, I'm here to take you on a relaxed, easy-to-understand journey that will lead you to the romantic success you desire. So, make yourself comfortable, and let's have some fun.

Who am I?

Before we dive into this exciting journey, you might be curious, "Who's this guy, and why should I listen to him when it comes to the art of connection?" That's a valid question, and I'm thrilled to introduce myself.

First and foremost, let's clarify who I am not: I'm not a psychologist, so please don't consider my advice as professional counsel. However, I do hold a degree in social sciences, which, despite some less-than-exciting lectures, equipped me with valuable insights into human nature and effective communication.

But what truly set me on this path was a simple desire: to gain the confidence and skills needed to approach and connect with women independently. I wanted the ability to strike up conversations, request phone numbers, arrange dates, or even share a memorable kiss, all with unwavering self-assurance, regardless of the circumstances.

So, I embarked on a journey of experimentation and self-improvement, and my passion for the art of seduction was ignited. I delved into every available resource, continuously refining my dating skills along the way.

The best part of this journey? I'm just an ordinary guy with a typical 9 to 5 job. I don't boast a Hollywood-worthy appearance, a supermodel physique, or a hefty bank account. What I do have is the knowledge of how to engage with women successfully, and I'm excited to share that knowledge with you.

If you're ready to join me on this adventure, let's dive right in!

Chapter 1
IDENTITY AND DESIRES

1. Your Identity, Your Perfect Match

Whether you're on the hunt for a long-term romance or just looking to dip your toes into the pool of casual encounters, I've got your back.

Picture this: you're walking down the street, and your heart goes wild when you spot that special someone. But hold on a second, before you go charging in like a love-struck bull, let's talk about finding the right person – the one who won't drive you crazy with her quirks or leave you wondering if you're speaking the same language.

Now, I won't pretend to be a love guru, but I've had my fair share of awkward dates and embarrassing rejections. I've learned that knowing who you are and what you want is like having a secret weapon in this crazy dating world. It's like bringing a map to a maze – trust me, you'll thank yourself later.

Alright, I hear you asking, "But what should I look for in a girl?" Well, my friend, that depends on you. Are you an adventurous soul looking for someone to climb mountains with? Or maybe you're more of a bookworm, seeking a partner to cozy up with on rainy days.

Here's the deal: there's no one-size-fits-all formula. Your perfect match might be the rebellious firecracker who challenges you to step out of your comfort zone, or perhaps it's the quiet, introverted type who cherishes peaceful evenings just as much as you do.

So, how do you find your ideal partner? Cue the drumroll, please. The first step is getting to know yourself – your passions, your pet peeves, and what makes you tick. Grab a notepad and jot down your quirks and qualities. Embrace them like badges of honor, for they will guide you to someone who truly appreciates the awesome human that you are.

In this section, we'll explore the wonders of compatibility – the stuff that keeps relationships sailing smoothly or might just steer you off course. We'll dive into the art of seeking similarities and shared values while leaving room for delightful differences that add spice to life.

Remember, my dear fellow love wanderer, this is no exact science. Love has its whims and wonders, but with a dash of humor, a pinch of self-awareness, and a sprinkle of open-heartedness, you'll be well on your way to discovering the magic of genuine connection.

So, let's embark on this quirky adventure of love and compatibility. Together, we'll unlock the secrets of finding that special someone who will have you laughing, swooning, and living your best blissful connection.

Did you grab your notebook? Great! Now create a list of your character traits, passions, things you like and don't like, lifestyles, etc. A good list should have two main chapters: Similarities and Behavior & Other Attributes.

❖Similarities

Under the "Similarities" category, jot down aspects related to your character traits, as well as your goals for relationships and life, along with your ethical principles. Now, let's discuss each of them:

◆ Character Traits

Let's say you are a guy with a great sense of humor and you meet a girl who'll be upset whenever you say something funny. Every time you'll have to apologize and tell her that it was just a joke. Consider how having such a girl in your life would be.

It is true that humor is relative, and what one person finds amusing, another may not understand or even find offensive. But believe me, there are women out there who don't understand humor at all. And in a relationship with a woman like that, only a man with no sense of humor can resist.

So, don't forget to write down all the character traits that you have. These may be adventurous, friendly, quiet, shy, introverted, extroverted, funny, serious, ambitious, optimistic, open-minded, devoted, reliable, etc. Then, seek out girls with similar characteristics.

◆ Relationship and Life Goals

Many factors contribute to a happy couple, but one of the most crucial is when both partners share common goals. Here are some examples of key relationship aspects and life goals that a couple should be aware of and work on together to foster harmony in their relationship:

◆ Type of Relationship and Family Planning

Both partners must be on the same page when it comes to relationship preferences or starting a family.

Examples:

Both partners enjoy being together, and they both want to start a family. This results in a happy couple.

Both partners enjoy being together, but they don't want to get married or have kids. This results in a happy couple.

If only one of the partners wants to get married or have kids while the other one doesn't, the partner who wants it will be very unhappy, and such a relationship is doomed to failure.

Now, let's say that you are interested only in one-night stands or friends with benefits type of relationships. In this case, you should try to find women who seek the same thing as you. There are plenty of women who don't want to involve themselves in classic relationships. There is no point in deceiving a girl who tells you right from the beginning that she wants a serious relationship. If you can't offer her what she wants, move on or be honest about your intentions. Some women, even if they want a serious relationship, may not wait without physical intimacy until they find someone who meets their requirements. So, you can be sincere and still have a physical relationship. For instance, if she asks you what you are looking for, and you are interested in one-night stands, you can say something like this: "I'm not looking for anything serious," or "Just seeing where things go." Regardless of your intentions, always respect the other person's boundaries and feelings. If someone is not interested in a casual relationship, don't pressure her or try to convince her otherwise.

◆ Relocation

It's not uncommon for couples to find themselves at a crossroads when it comes to moving to another country, state, or city. If you're contemplating a relocation soon, it's essential to be upfront with your date from the beginning. Let her know about your plans and intentions regarding the move. On the other hand, if you're content with where you are and have no plans to relocate, don't hesitate to ask your date if she ever envisions moving to another town or state.

◆ Trust and Respect

Trust and respect form the foundation of a strong relationship. Both partners should feel confident in each other's commitment and be respectful of each other's boundaries and individuality. When trust is lacking, it can lead to insecurity, doubts, and a breakdown in communication. Without trust, a relationship may become riddled with jealousy, suspicion, and misunderstandings, eroding the emotional connection that is so vital to its health and longevity.

◆ Communication

Open and honest communication is vital for any relationship. Couples should actively listen to each other, express their thoughts and feelings, and be receptive to each other's needs and concerns. If one partner's need or concern is ignored by the other, that may lead to misunderstandings, unmet expectations, and a lack of emotional connection, potentially impacting the relationship's overall health and longevity. Let's see some examples:

Example #1

Maya and James have just started dating, and they both come from different cultural backgrounds. Maya feels the need to discuss their cultural differences openly, understand each other's customs, and find ways to embrace and respect each other's traditions.

James is worried that talking about cultural differences might lead to conflict or misunderstandings. He avoids discussing it, assuming that their love will overcome any cultural barriers. However, this lack of communication leads to unintentional cultural insensitivity, which may create tension and resentment between them.

Example #2

Tom and Sarah have been dating for a few weeks, and Tom feels the need to discuss their boundaries regarding personal space and alone time. He wants to make sure they both feel comfortable and respected in their need for occasional solitude.

Sarah enjoys spending a lot of time together and fears that bringing up boundaries might suggest a lack of interest in the relationship. To avoid any potential conflict, Sarah doesn't talk about it. This results in Tom feeling suffocated and unable to recharge, causing tension and a potential strain on the relationship.

◆ Physical and Emotional Intimacy

Intimacy is a crucial aspect of a romantic relationship. Couples should be aware of each other's emotional and physical needs, and work together to maintain a fulfilling and affectionate connection.

These are not the only relationship goals but are the perfect examples. Other relationship or life goals might be Financial Goals, Career and Ambitions, Quality Time and Hobbies, Health and Wellness, Personal Growth, etc.

◆ Ethical Principles

Ethical principles differences can sometimes lead to conflicts and challenges in relationships, as individuals may have varying beliefs and values when it comes to moral decision-making. Here are some examples of ethical principles differences that may cause problems in a relationship:

- **Truthfulness and Honesty:** One partner highly values complete honesty and transparency in all matters, while the other believes in "white lies" to spare feelings or avoid conflicts.

- **Personal Finances:** One partner may be more inclined to take financial risks and live in the moment, while the other values frugality and long-term financial stability.

- **Animal Rights and Veganism:** One partner is passionate about animal rights and follows a strict vegan lifestyle, while the other does not share the same level of commitment to these principles.

- **Environmental Concerns:** One partner is deeply committed to environmental conservation and actively reduces waste, while the other is less concerned about environmental impact.

- **Religious Beliefs:** Partners may have different religious beliefs or levels of religiosity, leading to potential conflicts on matters such as religious practices, rituals, and how to raise children in the context of faith.

- **Euthanasia and Medical Decisions:** A couple may disagree on the ethical considerations of euthanasia or making difficult medical decisions for a loved one.

- **Lying vs. Protecting:** One partner may believe it's acceptable to withhold certain information to protect the other, while the other insists on complete truthfulness, even if it means facing difficult truths.

- **Capital Punishment:** A couple may hold opposing views on the morality of capital punishment, leading to heated debates on societal justice.

- **Privacy and Social Media:** One partner values privacy and avoids sharing personal information on social media, while the other is more open about their life online.

- **Abortion:** A couple may have differing beliefs about the moral implications of abortion, leading to significant emotional and philosophical clashes.

- **Gender Roles:** Traditional and modern views on gender roles within a relationship can lead to conflicts over household responsibilities, career choices, and parenting styles.

- **Corporate Responsibility:** One partner may prioritize supporting companies with ethical business practices, while the other may prioritize convenience and affordability.

- **Use of Technology:** A couple may have differing views on the ethical use of technology, such as the sharing of personal data or digital privacy.

- **Family Planning:** Ethical principles may influence decisions about family planning, including the use of contraception, fertility treatments, or the size of the family.

These ethical principles differences can be challenging to navigate, but open and respectful communication is crucial to finding common ground or agreeing to disagree on certain matters. It's essential for couples to discuss and understand each other's beliefs, values, and ethical perspectives.

You don't have to change your belief system to be with someone; you just have to respect other people's points of view. There are many couples where one partner is religious, and the other one is not, or one is affiliated with a political party, and the other one supports a different political party. So, for some couples, differences in beliefs are not a problem.

However, some people may feel very disappointed if their partner has different beliefs, but for some reason – probably because they're in love or don't want to lose that person – they accept it. That inevitably leads to conflicts later on.

If you find out that the girl you like holds different beliefs than you, and this upsets you a lot, then you might not be compatible with her. Consider staying with a girl who has different beliefs only if you are 100% sure that you're okay with it and, of course, she is okay with your beliefs as well.

Note: An important factor to clarify is that similarities should not be confused with commonalities. Liking the same food specialty, watching the same movie genre, or listening to the same music style, etc., are not similarities; they are commonalities.

Despite common conceptions that the majority of people have, commonalities are not essential for a relationship to work. Of course, it's great for both of you to have many things in common, but it's not a must-have. Disagreements over movie choices might lead to an argument aftermath affection, but when it comes to fundamental issues like having children, it could result in a breakup or divorce.

❖Behavior & Other Attributes

Each one of us has preferences and characteristics that others may like or dislike. Elements like looks, addictions, or certain lifestyles can become subjects of arguments later on. That's why it's better to identify behaviors and attributes in women that you may not feel comfortable with, as well as those you're willing to compromise on.

An important aspect to remember regarding this list is not to go overboard and write dozens of pages with a rigid checklist of what your future partner should have. However, don't ignore this list either. When it comes to finding a partner, there are two types of unlucky people: the overly picky type and the having no preferences at all type.

Being too picky may lead you to find something wrong with every potential date and result in a long period of loneliness. On the other hand, having no preferences at all might lead to choosing the wrong person, resulting in rejections, premature breakups, or toxic relationships. So, it's essential to strike a balance.

Take some time to create a reasonable list that reflects your core values and deal-breakers. While it may take a little effort now, it will save you a lot of trouble and heartache in the long run.

Q&A

Q: Does trying to hook up with a girl who seems right for me guarantee my success? Won't I be rejected?
A: I wish I could say yes, but unfortunately, I can't. Knowing who you are and what you want will improve your chances a lot, but there are no guarantees. An approach or an interaction could go wrong for various reasons that are not necessarily related to you.

Q: Will a relationship with a girl according to my list guarantee that no arguments and no breakups will occur?
A: I'm afraid not, but it will constitute a solid foundation. There are millions of reasons why a fight can start, but having a solid foundation increases the chances of reconciliation.

Conflicts are normal in any relationship, but how they are handled can make a significant difference. Couples should learn healthy ways to resolve conflicts, such as active listening, empathy, and compromise.

Q: How do I find a girl who has similar interests to mine?
A: While there is no sure-fire answer, here are some guidelines:
First, you need to **direct your searches** to environments where girls with similar interests as you are most likely to be. Look for girls that:

> ☿ **Works/study in the same or similar industry as you:** Often, people who end up forming a stable couple are those people with similarities such as working in the same field, having the same level of education, or same social status. For instance, both are doctors, both are lawyers, both are working in sales, both are working in the hospitality sector, etc. I understand that sometimes finding a woman in your field could be a challenge since there are different kinds of jobs,

some of them where the majority of employees are men, but you can still find someone with a similar profession. For instance, if you work in construction, you might find a girl who works in a fabric factory.

☼ **Have the same or similar lifestyle as you:** Lifestyle preferences are another important aspect when it comes to building a strong foundation for a potential relationship. For instance, if you frequently attend parties, nightclubs, and events, or enjoy a more carefree lifestyle, it is highly unlikely to resonate with a girl who spends most of her time in libraries, or with a more family-focused type of woman. So always take lifestyle into consideration in your searches. For example, if you are a fitness enthusiast who enjoys a healthy lifestyle and outdoor activities, you might be looking for a partner who either shares exactly the same interests and routines or someone who has a comparable lifestyle, perhaps focused on aerobics and health.

☼ **Are part of the same or similar community as you:** Searching for a potential girlfriend within your community is another way to find someone who shares your values and interests. Embrace the possibilities within your community, and you might discover a special connection that brings joy and fulfillment to your life. If you are not part of a community yet, join local groups or attend events related to your hobbies, and connect with like-minded individuals. Whether it's a book club, sports team, or volunteering opportunity, you increase the likelihood of finding a partner who appreciates you for who you are and shares your zest for life's adventures.

Next, **go with the flow.** After you find her, focus on getting to know her on a deeper level. If both of you are on the same page and the chemistry is right, things may naturally progress toward the relationship you want.

Deep conversations will be covered in Chapter 2. Till then, let's find out what characteristics women find attractive in a man and what elements are considered to be turn-offs.

2. Attraction's Green and Red Lights

What I have observed and pondered over time is that men who find themselves scratching their heads while interacting with women come in all shapes and sizes. Some may even have fancy degrees and an excellent vocabulary for using words like "confounding" and "bewildering." These are the very men that women claim they want when asked about their dream partner, yet they sometimes seem to get outshined by the infamous "bad boys." But fear not, dear perplexed gentlemen, for the puzzle of attraction, has many pieces.

Now, let's talk about those so-called "bad boys" – the ones who often act like they just stepped off the pages of a thrilling mystery novel. Women can't resist the allure of their confidence, the enigmatic aura they carry, and their daring spirit. It's as if they were equipped with a magnetic charm to draw attention effortlessly.

But hold your horses! Before you start donning a leather jacket and revving up a motorcycle, there's more to this story. The secret lies not in mimicking the "bad boy" persona but in embracing your own unique self. Remember, ladies appreciate the genuine article – a real deal with qualities like self-assurance, a touch of humor, and the ability to express emotions without resorting to broody stares.

So, here's the scoop: Women may have varied tastes like a smorgasbord of flavors, but what ultimately stands out is a dish called compatibility. Sprinkle in some good communication, a pinch of emotional intelligence, and a hearty serving of shared values – voilà! You have a recipe for meaningful connections.

In this section, we'll explore characteristics that generally tickle a woman's fancy and some that might raise a quizzical eyebrow.

Alright, listen up! These tidbits of knowledge might ring a bell for some of you, like that one catchy tune you just can't get out of your head. But hey, even a seasoned expert can use a friendly nudge – consider it a delightful refresher course! Remember, learning and understanding can bridge gaps even better than a pickup line (unless it's a really, really good one – I'm talking a real zinger).

☺Turn-Ons

When it comes to men, every woman has her unique preferences, making it impossible to cover every aspect here. Each woman is wonderfully different, and what one finds attractive, another might not. However, fear not, dear readers, for I'll be focusing on those characteristics that are widely adored by many women. These magical traits are what we call "turn-ons."

👍 Inner Strength

If you were to stroll down the street and ask any woman what she desires most in a man, many would say, "Strength." But let's clarify, they're not talking about bulging muscles or feats of physical prowess. No, what they truly seek is mental and emotional strength.

For women, a strong man is one with a solid character, a clear sense of self, and a firm grasp on his life's purpose. They are drawn to someone who exudes calmness and confidence, someone who doesn't feel the need to prove themselves to the world, as they already know their worth. A man who navigates life's hurdles with ease, rather than someone who seeks constant approval or complains at the slightest obstacle.

So, be strong, not weak! Weakness, in the form of insecurities, neediness, and self-doubt, can quickly dampen a woman's interest. An unsure demeanor and a lack of self-assurance can sabotage any chance of attraction.

Remember, women often have many options, so they won't invest their time in emotionally unstable men or those who resort to shallow tactics just to win them over.

In essence, cultivate your inner strength, and let your genuine confidence shine through. That's the kind of strength that will draw women to you, like moths to a flame.

👍 Confidence

One of the most attractive qualities in a man is undeniably confidence. It's a trait that holds universal appeal to women. Yet, it's perfectly normal for many guys to struggle with confidence at times. Life experiences, past setbacks, or unkind words from others can chip away at our self-assurance. But here's the great news – confidence can be regained, no matter what caused its temporary absence.

The first step towards building your confidence is accepting and embracing who you are while remaining open to self-improvement. Recognize your flaws and work on fixing what you can. For those aspects you cannot change, remember the "SO WHAT" mindset (we'll delve into this later in the book) and focus on areas where you can grow. For instance, shedding a few extra pounds is achievable with discipline, but height isn't something you can change. Nevertheless, you can elevate your attitude, and with the right mindset, you can flourish in the dating scene, regardless of your appearance.

The second step involves adopting the demeanor of a confident person. You've probably heard the saying, "Fake it till you make it," which holds some truth. You can begin by imitating the actions of confident individuals in social situations.

Confident people exude determination, boldness, maintain eye contact, display good posture, and speak clearly. They firmly believe in their self-worth. We'll explore these aspects further along the way. For now, remember that by being comfortable with who you are and emulating the behaviors of confident individuals, you'll be perceived as a confident guy.

Embrace the journey of self-assurance, and you'll discover that confidence becomes not only attractive to others but also a valuable asset in all aspects of your life.

👍 Individuality

Another captivating trait that women adore in a man is individuality. Throughout time, women have been drawn to guys who embrace their uniqueness and those who stand out in their own special ways. Now, let's revisit the self-analysis you conducted (yes, I hope you did!), and identify those qualities that make you different, special, or unique. Once you've pinpointed them, it's time to accentuate and showcase these distinctive attributes.

Individuality can take various forms – it might be your personal style, a sport you excel in, a life philosophy you hold dear, a special talent or ability, a passionate pursuit, or even a captivating hobby. The key is to present something understandable and appealing, avoiding any awkward or embarrassing situations. After all, it's crucial to be unique in the right way.

For example, having a distinctive personal style is fantastic, but veering into outdated fashion choices might not be the best idea. Strive to channel your uniqueness through modern and tasteful expressions that speak volumes about your personality and preferences.

👍 Ambition

Now, let me unveil the captivating allure of ambition and how it becomes a sizzling turn-on for women! Picture this – you, the hero of your own story, setting sail on the sea of dreams, with ambition as your trusty compass, guiding you towards the land of success and fulfillment.

In this grand journey of relationships, ambition is like a shining beacon that draws others to you like magnets to metal. It's that special spark that ignites a fire within, signaling to the world that you're a go-getter, a dream chaser, and a force to be reckoned with!

When you embrace ambition, you become a magnet of inspiration — like a glowing lighthouse on a stormy night, guiding ships to safe shores. Women can't resist this charismatic energy, for ambition is the elixir of growth, the catalyst for greatness.

Imagine yourself as a captivating protagonist, driven by purpose and passion, charting your course amidst life's challenges. Ambition isn't just about wanting to conquer the world; it's about unyielding dedication to your goals, like an artist crafting a masterpiece stroke by stroke.

When you walk the path of ambition, you become an architect of your destiny, designing a life that's extraordinary and fulfilling. Women are like ardent explorers, drawn to the thrill of adventure, and your ambition promises them a journey of a lifetime.

But, my dear dreamer, remember that ambition isn't a solo mission; it's an invitation for others to join you on your epic quest. Be open to collaboration, like a skillful conductor leading an orchestra of talent toward harmonious symphonies.

As you chase your dreams, share your vision with others, and be receptive to their aspirations as well. Ambition is the language of possibility, and women long to be part of a shared vision, like co-authors of a beautiful love story.

However, a word of caution — balance your ambition with empathy and understanding. Like a gentle gardener tending to a flourishing garden, nurture your relationships and support your partner's dreams too.

So, my fellow adventurer, embrace your ambition with zest, let it fuel your pursuits, and watch as it weaves a spell of fascination around you. Be the hero of your story, and let ambition be the enchanting melody that entices women to join you in creating a life of boundless possibilities!

👍 Integrity

Ah, my curious seeker of love, let me unveil the mystical secret of why integrity is a blazing beacon of attraction for women! Picture this – you, standing tall like a majestic lighthouse, radiating authenticity and truthfulness. That, my friend, is the irresistible allure of integrity!

In this magical realm of relationships, integrity is the golden key that unlocks the gates to trust and emotional connection. When you embody integrity, you become a magnetic force, drawing others towards you like bees to honey.

Imagine yourself as the protagonist of a grand adventure, and integrity is your noble quest. It's the hero's virtue that stands unwavering in the face of temptation and deceit. Women are drawn to integrity, captivated by its representation of a solid moral foundation – a rock to lean on, a compass guiding you toward righteousness.

Integrity is a gem that gleams brightly, reflecting your inner character, and women can't resist its brilliance. It's like savoring a delectable dish prepared with the finest ingredients; integrity leaves a lasting impression that lingers on the taste buds of the heart.

When you walk the path of integrity, you become a trustworthy confidante, a pillar of support, and a safe harbor in the stormy seas of life. It's like being the wise mentor in a hero's journey – someone women can count on to champion their dreams and protect their hearts.

But remember my dear seeker of truth, integrity is not a mask to be worn when convenient. It's an unwavering commitment to be your authentic self, even when the world tempts you to sway. Women are like skilled treasure hunters; they can spot the real gem from a mile away.

Embrace integrity as your guiding star, and you'll find yourself on a path of profound connection and genuine love. So, venture forth with valor, my friend, and let integrity be your shining armor – the radiant source of genuine attraction that captivates the hearts of women and leads you to the grandest of adventures!

👍 Trustworthy

Let's reveal now the enchanting magic of trustworthiness and why it becomes an irresistible turn-on for women! Picture this: you, standing tall like a solid oak tree, with trustworthiness as your mighty roots, grounding you in authenticity and reliability.

In the realm of relationships, trustworthiness is the sacred elixir that nurtures love and fosters a profound connection. When you embody trustworthiness, you become a beacon of security and dependability, drawing others to you like bees to nectar.

Imagine yourself as the hero of a grand saga, and trustworthiness is your noble quest. It's the knight's shining armor, shielding you from doubts and suspicions. Women are captivated by this radiant armor, for trustworthiness is the fortress of emotional safety.

When you walk the path of trustworthiness, you become a reliable confidant, a steadfast partner, and a guardian of promises. Women can't resist this majestic aura, for trustworthiness is the currency of loyalty, the treasure of emotional intimacy.

But beware, my dear guardian of trust, for trustworthiness is not a fleeting act, but a way of being. Let your actions speak louder than words, like a lyrical symphony that weaves harmony into relationships.

Embrace honesty like a beacon in the darkness, illuminating the path of truth. Be accountable for your actions like a wise sage, for trustworthiness requires ownership of your mistakes and the courage to make amends.

Let empathy flow from your heart like a healing river, nurturing emotional bonds with tenderness and understanding. Trustworthiness is the art of keeping promises like a skilled painter, creating a masterpiece of reliability.

In the world of love and connection, trustworthiness reigns as the crown jewel, elevating you to a pedestal of admiration and respect. Cherish the treasure of trust, for it is the foundation upon which love thrives.

So, my dear seeker of trustworthiness, walk the path with unwavering devotion, and you shall discover the most profound connection and a love that withstands the trials of time.

May your heart be the sanctuary of trust, and may your relationships bloom with the enchanting fragrance of unwavering loyalty. With trustworthiness as your guiding star, you shall become a beacon of love that shines brighter than any constellation in the universe of relationships!

👍 Mystery

Ah, dear reader, let me unveil the captivating enigma of mystery and why it holds the power to ignite sparks of attraction in women! Picture this: you, a charming enchanter, shrouded in an aura of allure and fascination. The art of embracing mystery is like a secret potion, a delicate balance between revealing and concealing, that keeps her curiosity piqued and her heart intrigued.

In the realm of relationships, mystery is the art of unveiling your story one tantalizing chapter at a time. It's like a thrilling novel that keeps her eagerly turning the pages, captivated by the journey of discovery. Embrace this intriguing dance, and watch as she falls under your spell, drawn to the allure of the unknown.

But first, allow me to clarify: being mysterious, doesn't entail deceit or concealing vital aspects from her. Embracing the allure of mystery means exercising caution when revealing too much about yourself too soon. It's essential to resist the urge to spill your life's story to a woman right from the beginning, even if she curiously probes for more personal details. Timing is everything. While you can answer her questions, it's wise to be mindful of what you share.

Avoid delving into problems or negative experiences prematurely. Remember, there's always a chance of saying something she may not be ready to hear.

Intrigue her by letting her uncover fascinating facets of your life through other sources, such as social media or word-of-mouth. Women enjoy a bit of investigative work, and they may likely take to Google to learn more about you or peruse your social media profiles. Now is an opportune time to give your profiles a friendly inspection and eliminate any content that could cast you in an unfavorable light.

Think of yourself as a treasure chest, filled with captivating stories waiting to be discovered. As you reveal intriguing tidbits about yourself over time, you build a sense of anticipation and excitement. Like a skilled magician, you leave her wanting more, eager to delve deeper into the enigma that is you.

So, my dear enchanter of mystery, let the dance of revelation begin. Embrace the art of gradual disclosure, and watch as she becomes entranced by the allure of the unknown. With each chapter of your story unveiled, you build a bond that is bound to withstand the test of time, for true attraction lies not only in what is revealed but also in what remains enticingly concealed.

👍 Humor

If you ever seek advice from seasoned guys on how to charm women, one answer is bound to come up: "Make her laugh!" And you might wonder, "Why do I have to make her laugh? Am I supposed to be a clown?" Fear not, you're no clown, but let me pose a question: When do you feel your best? Is it during dull interactions or those moments filled with laughter? Laughter, my friend, is the key to feeling good, and it doesn't require you to be a buffoon. You see, it's not about being a clown but about infusing some humor into your interactions, showing her that being with you is an enjoyable and fun experience.

In the realm of relationships, humor is the key that unlocks a treasure trove of joyful experiences. It's like a melody that resonates with the heart, bringing forth laughter and genuine happiness. Embrace this enchanting gift, and watch as she becomes spellbound by the delightful world you create together.

Humor can be your secret weapon, compensating for any perceived shortcomings. Even if you don't consider yourself the most attractive or physically fit guy, a great sense of humor can work wonders with women.

Now, I must admit that being funny is something that can't be taught easily. It often depends on one's nature and personality. However, in the upcoming chapters, I'll provide you with some examples of what funny interactions with women might look like, giving you a good idea of how to infuse humor into your interactions.

Making her laugh will make her feel good, and she'll thank you for it later. Just two things to keep in mind:

First, don't overuse it; hit the pause button from time to time. You want her to see that you can handle a meaningful talk, not that you are a human punchline.

Second, try to avoid laughing excessively at your own jokes. While it's perfectly fine to enjoy your own humor, be mindful of the frequency and intensity of your laughter. Constantly laughing at your own jokes might give the impression that you're seeking validation or attention, which can be off-putting. A genuine smile is enough for her to recognize your humor and appreciate the light-hearted connection.

So, dear purveyor of laughter, let the comedy show begin! Embrace the power of humor, and you'll find yourself sprinkling stardust of joy into your interactions. With each well-timed jest, you create a symphony of laughter that binds hearts and sparks connections. Remember, my friend, in this grand tale of love, humor is the magic spell that leaves her enchanted and longing for more.

👍 Smiling

Now, my dear seeker of meaningful connections, let me illuminate the enchanting power of your smile and why it serves as your secret weapon to weave a tapestry of genuine relationships. Picture this: you lock eyes with someone across the room, and in that fleeting moment, something magical happens. Your smile lights up your face, sending a subtle but powerful message. In an instant, you've conveyed warmth, openness, and a genuine interest in connecting with the other person. Smiling when trying to connect to someone isn't just a reflex; it's an art that can transform social interactions in incredible ways.

So, why does this simple act of smiling hold so much significance? Let's delve into the fascinating reasons why a smile can be your secret weapon for creating meaningful connections:

- ☆ **A Welcoming Aura:** Like a beacon of approachability, your smile signals to others that you're friendly, approachable, and ready to engage.
- ☆ **Leaving a Lasting Impression:** Ever heard of a smile being worth a thousand words? It's true! Your beaming expression can etch a positive memory of you in the minds of those you meet.
- ☆ **Silent Communication:** When words fail, a smile speaks volumes. It communicates respect, acknowledgment, and a genuine interest in the other person.
- ☆ **Forging Bonds:** Think of your smile as a bridge that connects you with others. By smiling, you lay the foundation for building rapport and genuine connections.
- ☆ **A Contagious Spark:** Just like laughter, smiles are contagious. Your radiant grin encourages others to reciprocate, creating a harmonious and uplifting atmosphere.
- ☆ **Easing Tensions:** Intense eye contact can sometimes feel intimidating, but a smile can work wonders in melting away

tension, making interactions more comfortable.

☆ **Unlocking Social Superpowers:** A genuine smile show-cases your emotional intelligence and social prowess, making you more likable, empathetic, and socially adept.

So, the next time you find yourself around girls, remember the power of your smile. It's not just a reflexive facial gesture; it's a captivating tool that can enchant and delight, leaving a trail of positive connections wherever you go.

It's important to note that smiling should be genuine and respectful. Forced or insincere smiles can be perceived as disingenuous or manipulative. So, when you interact or make eye contact with anyone, including a woman, a genuine smile can go a long way in creating positive interactions and building meaningful connections. However, always be mindful of cultural differences and individual preferences, as some people may interpret smiling differently based on their background or personal experiences.

Now, armed with the wisdom of your smile, go forth, dear seeker, and illuminate the world with the magic of your genuine connections!

👍 The Look

Now, it's time to unleash the power of "The Look" and boost your dating game to a whole new level. Let's dive into the three game-changing elements: Dressing, Haircuts, and Hygiene.

Dressing – Lookin' Fly and Oh-So-Spry! When it comes to dressing, remember, there's no one-size-fits-all approach. But fear not, I've got some sharp and witty guidelines to help you navigate the fashion jungle:

Wear clothes that suit your age, body type, and handsome features. You want to be a head-turner, not a head-scratcher!

Get that fit on point – not too tight, not too loose. Your clothes should be as tailor-made as your charm.

Dress like a chameleon – adapt to any situation! Be ready to rock casual, formal, or party vibes. I've got you covered!

Keep your threads clean and pristine. Stains, odors, and wrinkles are a no-go zone! We don't want you scaring off the ladies with fashion faux pas.

However, mind that just because a particular outfit is on trend doesn't automatically mean it's the perfect fit for everyone. It's essential to consider your unique style, personality, comfort, and physiognomy when selecting your clothes. Authenticity always shines, and when you choose items that complement your individuality and physiognomy, you'll always look your best.

Haircuts – Unleash the Hair-mazing! Time to tame that mane, gents! Your haircut is like a secret weapon, but there's no one-size-fits-all here either. Here's my buzzworthy advice:

Experiment and discover your signature style. Don't be afraid to mix it up and impress with your unique charm.

Find a top-notch barber and let him work his magic. Trust me, the right cut can turn you into a heartthrob.

So, stay trendy but be true to yourself. Rock that hairstyle like it's the hottest thing on the catwalk!

Hygiene – The Squeaky-Clean Seduction: Alright, guys, I know this is basic stuff, but it's essential. Good hygiene is the backbone of attraction, so let's scrub up and shine bright:

Show some love to your grooming routine. A clean and well-groomed man is a magnet for ladies.

Remember, fresh breath is a lifesaver! So minty-fresh is the way to go.

Stay suave with good personal hygiene. Your confidence will sky-rocket, and the ladies will take notice.

There you have it, gentlemen – the trifecta of awesomeness, "The

Look" edition! By nailing your dressing, haircuts, and hygiene game, you'll radiate confidence and irresistible charm. Go out there, rock your swagger, and let the ladies come to you! Happy dating!

☹ Turn-offs

Ah, the dating game! We've all been there, stumbling upon those moments when our best intentions seem to take a sudden detour into the realm of unintentional mistakes. You know the ones – those cringe-worthy actions or words that leave women instantly uninterested. Yes, my fellow gentlemen, we've experienced those relationship roadblocks firsthand, and they're what we call "turn-offs."

In this section, we'll dive into those all-too-familiar dating faux pas and uncover the common behaviors or traits that can cool a woman's interest faster than ice in Antarctica. It's not a matter of being perfect or holding an exhaustive list of do's and don'ts, but rather recognizing and learning from those missteps. So, let's navigate the treacherous waters of dating with newfound self-awareness and understanding. Together, we'll steer clear of the turn-offs and set sail for smoother seas in our pursuit of lasting connections.

👎 Being Desperate

Picture this: you meet an incredible woman, and you can't help but feel a rush of excitement and attraction. It's natural to want her to know how much she means to you, but tread carefully, my friend. The road to a woman's heart isn't paved with desperation, and steering clear of this pitfall is crucial. As men, we must be mindful of the common behaviors that can send women running for the hills, labeling us as desperate or clingy. After all, no one wants to be perceived that way in the dating world.

So, let's explore some typical traits of a desperate guy and learn how to avoid falling into this unattractive category:

💣 **Showing too much interest:** While showing genuine interest is essential, bombarding her with excessive attention can be overwhelming. Remember, it's all about balance. Avoid being too eager or available, as this might stifle her opportunity to develop authentic feelings. If you find yourself constantly trying to please her, showering her with compliments, or suffocating her with texts and calls, it's time to step back and allow her the space to miss you.

💣 **Appearing devoid of personal preferences or opinions:** It's a common misconception that agreeing with everything she says or pretending to like everything she likes will win her over. In reality, showcasing your unique opinions and preferences can be more appealing. Be true to yourself and don't shy away from respectfully expressing your differences. A reasonable woman will appreciate your authenticity and admire your confidence.

💣 **Rushing things:** Trying to speed up the natural progress of a relationship can be a deal breaker too. The initial stages of attraction are indeed a time when swift action is beneficial. When you first notice her and feel that spark, don't hesitate to strike up a conversation. Taking the initiative early on is essential, as it demonstrates your interest and prevents missed opportunities. If you delay, someone else might seize the chance, and you could miss out on a wonderful connection. Once you're dating, let things unfold at their own pace. If she's genuinely interested, she'll stick around.

In short, desperation is a dating downfall that we must avoid at all costs. It's an unattractive trait that can send potential connections fleeing. If you've noticed a sudden change in her interest level, it might be time to reassess your approach and ensure you're steering clear of any signs of desperation.

Now that we've navigated this treacherous territory, let's

embrace a more confident and balanced approach to dating. By doing so, we'll enhance our appeal and set the stage for genuine and lasting connections.

✍ Threats or Ultimatums

The golden rule here is elegantly simple: just don't. Under no circumstances should you ever push a woman into a corner where she's forced to choose between "X" (your preference) and "Y" (what's been bothering you), unless you're a fan of unpleasant surprises. You see, men and women often have different perspectives on such matters. While men might view an ultimatum from a woman as a logical step, the reverse can introduce unnecessary stress and tension into a relationship, often leading to heated arguments, escalation of conflicts, or simply radio silence followed by a breakup.

A humorous friend of mine has a catchphrase, "When dealing with women, do the opposite of what you think is right." Of course, this is all in jest, but it playfully underscores the idea that what may seem logical to us, guys, can sometimes have the opposite effect on women.

When you find that the person you're dating exhibits behavior that doesn't quite align with your expectations, it's imperative to engage in an internal dialogue. Consider whether the issue at hand truly holds the weight of a "make or break" moment in your interaction or relationship. Is it a matter of deep-seated values or an essential boundary for you? Or is it something that, in the grand scheme of your connection, falls within the realm of compromise and understanding?

Dating and relationships are an intricate dance of give and take, where both partners bring their unique perspectives and experiences. What might seem paramount to you could be viewed differently by your partner. In such cases, it's often more fruitful to initiate an open and honest conversation. Share your feelings, concerns, and desires without resorting to ultimatums or threats. This approach can pave the way for mutual understanding and compromise, fostering a healthier and more harmonious relationship.

In the rare instances where an ultimatum becomes unavoidable, ensure it's based on a fundamental value or boundary that you cannot compromise on. Even then, deliver it with utmost care and empathy, keeping in mind that your goal is not to corner your partner but to communicate your needs while respecting hers. Forcing someone into making a decision out of fear or guilt rather than genuine desire is not a healthy way to maintain a relationship.

👎 Staring

Ah, the pearls of wisdom from my old man, "Look but don't stare" – his sage advice for the precarious world of women! Of course, it applies to everyone, really, because no one wants to be on the receiving end of a full-on staring contest. But, when it comes to charming the ladies, a subtle approach is your best wingman.

See, staring can land you in "creepyville" or "awkwardsville," and those are not ideal destinations for any aspiring Casanova. So, let's learn the art of eye contact, shall we?

Start with glances – think of it as a flirtatious dance of the eyes. Catch her gaze and hold it for a few seconds, then nonchalantly shift your focus elsewhere. Now, don't be looking up like you've seen a celestial marvel or down like you've misplaced your courage. That'll send the wrong signals, my friend!

For counting the seconds, here's a trick: "One Mississippi, Two Mississippi." If she looks away before "Two Mississippi," don't fret, give it another shot later. If she maintains eye contact beyond that, well, well, looks like you've piqued her curiosity. More than two seconds, and you've got yourself a potential admirer; less than that, and it might be time to softly retreat.

Now, shy girls might not be the masters of prolonged eye contact

— they might avert their gaze quickly, like a timid butterfly fluttering away. But here's the twist — they can still sneak a peek at you a few moments later like a curious cat cautiously returning to check things out.

So, keep your detective hat on! If you notice a shy damsel looking away but then stealing glances your way, it could be a sign that she's secretly intrigued. These delicate dance moves of the eyes can be quite perplexing, but fear not my friend, it's all part of the intricate game of attraction.

And remember, a genuine smile can work wonders — it's like an all-purpose charm offensive! So, flash those pearly whites and watch the magic unfold.

Ah, I almost forgot the secret art of timing! Here's a golden tip for you, my friend: When engaged in this subtle game of eye contact, let her make the first move. Yes, you heard it right — no need to be hasty! Wait until she gracefully shifts her gaze away before you follow suit.

It's like a captivating dance, where you lead by example but graciously let her set the pace. You see, if you keep gazing even after she's moved on, it might come across as a touch too eager. And we certainly don't want that, do we?

So, when her eyes take a little detour, go ahead and shift your focus too. It's all about the art of finesse and mirroring her cues, like a suave charmer who knows the rhythm of the tango.

Remember, patience is a virtue in matters of the heart, and in this game of glances, a well-timed step can lead to a delightful connection. Happy waltzing with your eyes, my fellow Romeo!

Now, what if you're already in the throes of conversation, say, on a first date? Resist the temptation to ogle, my friend. Instead, opt for regular eye contact to keep the connection alive and kicking.

But, if you want to be sneaky like a secret agent on a mission, there's always the peripheral vision technique. Imagine, stealthily using your side vision to survey the surroundings, just like a ninja assessing the battlefield. Armed with your laptop, or phone, or even while chatting with friends, you can discreetly keep an eye on the ladies. Don't worry; they won't know you've got your "spy specs" on!

So, to sum it up, it's all about subtlety and finesse – the kind that would make even James Bond raise an impressed eyebrow. Remember, the eyes have it, but use your powers wisely.

And remember, every girl has her unique way of expressing interest, so keep your radar tuned, and you just might unlock the enigmatic code of her affections. Happy hunting, and may the charms be with you!

Inappropriate Touches

The unwritten rules of physical contact – pinching, grabbing, or slapping – let's face it, those moves are guaranteed to score you a one-way ticket to the "Hostile Feelings Land." And trust me, you don't want to be their mayor!

Women appreciate respect, and nothing says "I respect you" less than making them feel like an unwilling participant in a wrestling match. Intimidating or degrading moves are a big no-no, my friend. It's like stepping on a landmine of discomfort, and that's not the kind of explosive chemistry you're after.

But fear not, oh seeker of connections! There's a touchy-feely side that doesn't involve crossing boundaries. Innocent touches are like the seasoning of your interactions – just a pinch here and a dash there to add flavor to the conversation.

For example, when you're passionately recounting a school story, you can gracefully take her hand to show how the teacher once guided you out of the classroom. It's like a theatrical gesture that will make your tale come alive, and it won't land you in detention!

Or picture this – playfully challenging her story with a "Come on, I don't believe you!" while giving her a gentle push with your fingertips. It's like a friendly nudge that says, "I'm interested, but I'm not easily fooled."

Now, before you start mapping out your touch strategy, remember to keep it natural and justified. You don't want to look like you're doing hand gymnastics just to impress her. Subtle touches on the forearm or shoulder while expressing your thoughts can be smooth as silk.

And timing, my dear friend, is everything. Start introducing these innocent touches early on, like sprinkling them as you're cooking up a delicious connection. Because if you suddenly go all "touchy-feely" after half an hour, it might raise a few eyebrows and create a moment as awkward as a penguin trying to dance salsa.

Perhaps you're wondering why these playful pokes and subtle touches hold such significance. Well, they're not just there to add flavor to the conversation; they're the secret sauce for when you're ready to take things up a notch, like holding hands or going in for a smooch. These early, playful touches, done right, act as a form of non-verbal communication, instilling comfort and rapport. So, when the stars align and it's time for the big move, the transition becomes a seamless and authentic progression.

Now, here's the touchy-feely rulebook – avoid anything below the belt or buttocks until you've built a cozy comfort zone or shared an intimate connection. Until then, keep it light, keep it playful, and watch those sparks fly! Happy touching, but remember, always touch responsibly!

👇 Trying to Impress

Behold the classic "trying to impress women" escapade – a well-intentioned but often misguided journey. Picture this, my fellow travelers: men donning their finest peacock feathers, strutting about, hoping to catch the eye of the elusive lady. But, lo and behold, the truth we must uncover is this – genuine charm reigns supreme!

Yes, ladies and gentlemen, it's the real you that'll sweep them off their feet, not some flashy smoke and mirrors act. So, let's take a detour and explore why trying to impress in an insincere way might land you in the "Oops, that didn't work" territory:

First stop – the **Needy Impression** station. Beware, for attempting to impress might unwittingly trigger the "Emergency Neediness Siren." Desperation to fill a void might sneak up on you like an unexpected surprise party – and trust me, nobody wants that kind of surprise

Next up – **Unrealistic Expectations** central! By aiming to impress, you might set the bar so high that even an Olympic pole vaulter would have a hard time clearing it. And when reality shows up like a grouchy Monday morning, disappointment follows suit.

Onward we go, passing the **Missed Connections** junction! Focusing solely on impressing means you might miss out on the opportunity to genuinely connect. It's like buying a ticket to the grand symphony but plugging your ears – the beautiful music is right there, waiting for you to embrace it!

And last but not least, we arrive at the **Lack of Emotional Connection** hub. Impressions built on superficial acts might lead to relationships as deep as a kiddie pool. Sure, it's fun for a splash, but not ideal for a long, meaningful swim.

So, dear passengers of the love train, let's agree – no need for theatrical performances or borrowed identities. Instead, let's take the path of authentic connections, where honest communication, shared interests, and genuine appreciation for each other reign supreme.

Remember, when you're true to yourself, love might just tap you on the shoulder and say, "Hey there, fancy meeting you here!" So, leave the masks at the door, folks, and let your unique charm shine through! Safe travels, and may the Cupid's arrows be ever in your favor!

Nervous Laugh

The nervous laugh – that mysterious phenomenon that leaves us all scratching our heads and wondering, "What in the world was that about?" It's like a surprise guest at a party, showing up uninvited and making everyone go, "Huh?"

But fear not, my fellow laughologists! Let's decode the secrets of the nervous laugh, especially when it comes to those captivating creatures called women. Brace yourselves for some laughter analysis!

Picture this: You're in the middle of a serious discussion, and out of nowhere, that nervous laughter decides to make an appearance, like an unexpected party crasher. Now, don't get me wrong, laughter is a fantastic icebreaker, but timing is key, my friend!

Spotting the nervous laugh in action is like playing detective. Look for signs like inappropriate timing, excessive chuckles, tense body language, and a voice that might sound like a squirrel on helium. It's like a laughter treasure hunt!

Now, here's the thing – while that nervous giggle might be your trusty armor against the stress monsters, it can lead to some unintended side effects in social interactions, especially with the ladies. Authenticity is the name of the game, and the nervous laugh might just raise a few authenticity alarms.

Imagine this – you're trying to communicate your true feelings, but that laugh-o-meter is going haywire, sending mixed signals faster than a lost GPS. No worries, though! Here are some strategies to help you tame that laughter beast.

- First off, **self-awareness** is your trusty sidekick. Be aware of when and why nervous laughter tends to occur. Recognize those trigger situations and patterns, like a laugh-themed scavenger hunt, as it will help you identify patterns and work towards addressing them.
- Next, **practice some self-acceptance:** Understand that it's natural to experience nerves or anxiety in certain situations, and it's okay to feel vulnerable, like a marshmallow in a world of s'mores. Accepting yourself and your emotions without judgment can reduce the need for nervous

laughter as a defense mechanism.

⚒ **Activate your inner listening guru!** Instead of juggling thoughts about how you appear, give the ladies your full attention. It's like having a secret weapon – genuine conversations that make self-consciousness disappear!

⚒ **Humor with intention:** If you use humor as a coping mechanism, make sure it's like a finely crafted joke – light-hearted and appropriate for the situation, rather than laughter used solely to mask discomfort. And remember, laughing at your own jokes might raise a few eyebrows, so avoid it.

⚒ **Calling all laughter superheroes!** If those nervous chuckles are still running the show, don't hesitate to bring in the big guns – a therapist or counselor! They'll help you unravel the mystery behind the laughter and equip you with personalized coping strategies. It's like having your very own laughter avengers!

But hey, I get it – nervous laughter might always be a quirky part of who you are, and that's perfectly fine! The goal is to manage it like a laugh guru, using other coping mechanisms when the situation calls for it.

So, there you have it, my laugh-loving friends! Embrace the giggles, tame the chuckles, and remember, genuine connections are the real belly laughers of life. Happy laughing, with intention, of course!

👎 Sending Mixed Signals

The classic mixed signals conundrum. You know what they say: "If you're going to send signals, make sure they're coming from the same transmission tower!" Sending mixed signals can be like navigating a maze blindfolded – confusing and hilarious (but not in a good way).

For the ladies, as for everyone else, it's like playing a game of emotional charades. One moment, they're guessing "interested," and the next, it's "disinterested." It's like trying to figure out a Rubik's Cube with the lights off – a real puzzler!

Picture this: someone's into you today, and then they disappear faster than a magician's rabbit. Now you see 'em, now you don't! Abracadabra, huh? It's enough to leave you scratching your head like you've just encountered a mind-boggling magic trick.

Consistency is the name of the game, folks! When the signals are all over the place, it's like watching a quirky dance routine. The cha-cha today, the tango tomorrow, and the chicken dance the day after! It's like they're moonwalking through emotions.

In the realm of love and relationships, honesty and clarity reign supreme. It's like aiming for the bullseye in Cupid's dartboard. If you can't hit the target with your feelings, you might end up in a tangled mess, and nobody wants that – unless it's a game of Twister!

So, dear friends, let's keep the mixed signals at bay and embrace straightforwardness like a comforting hug. Being genuine and open with our feelings is like serving a delicious dish of trust and understanding. And let's face it, who doesn't love a good dish of emotional authenticity?

In conclusion, sending mixed signals can be quite the roller-coaster ride – thrilling, confusing, and sometimes even funny. But when it comes to matters of the heart, being honest and clear with our intentions is the secret sauce to forming a meaningful connection. So, let's ditch the confusing charades and go for heartfelt communication – it's a win-win, like getting the high score on an emotional pinball machine!

👎 Being Romantic Too Soon

The magic of movies. They whisk us away to dreamy worlds filled with fairy-tale romances, where love sprouts faster than a garden of roses. But hold on tight, my fellow romantics, because reality might not be ready for our blockbuster love stories just yet!

In these cinematic wonders, characters confess their undying love with epic monologues that make Shakespeare jealous. They sweep their love interests off their feet with impulsive gestures that even Cupid would envy. It's like a love express train, racing to the happily-ever-after station at full speed!

But let's press pause on our movie reel for a moment. As we venture into the real world, we must beware of the "too much, too soon" romantic frenzy! You see, my friends, rushing into romance like a toddler in a candy store might not always get us the sweet results we crave.

Imagine this – showering someone with extravagant gifts or proclaiming undying love after just a few dates. It's like proposing with fireworks on the first date – exhilarating, but possibly overwhelming! Let's save the fireworks display for the grand finale, shall we?

And don't even get me started on social media overdrive! Tagging the person in a dozen lovey-dovey posts before the relationship has even taken off is like going from 0 to 100 in the love lane. Slow and steady wins the love race, my dear friends!

Now, I'm not saying to ditch romance altogether – that would be like removing sprinkles from a donut – a crime against love and sweetness! Instead, let's savor the journey like sipping fine wine and letting the flavors unfold.

Take it easy with the constant messages and calls – it's like a love marathon, and we don't want to run out of breath before we reach the finish line! Healthy boundaries are like the seat belts that keep us safe on this love rollercoaster.

So, dear romantics, let's embrace the magic of movies but remember that real-life love is like a delicious slow-cooked meal – it takes time, effort, and a dash of patience. With a sprinkle of genuine connection, a pinch of mutual understanding, and a dollop of respect, we'll cook up a love story that stands the test of time! Bon appétit!

👎Declaring Your Feelings Before You Start Dating Her

The classic movie clichés strike again – that ever-present line, "If you love her, you should tell her!" Trust me, I've lost count of how many times that sappy advice has graced the silver screen. But hold your popcorn, my friends, because there's a little problem with the timing here!

You see, in movie magic, characters are advised to declare their love faster than a bullet train – even if they've barely had a chat about the weather! It's like trying to build a sandcastle without any sand – not the best foundation, right?

Picture this: our hero falls head over heels for his colleague, and all they've ever talked about is TPS reports and office gossip. Or he's madly in love with a coffee shop waitress, and their only exchange is a simple "more coffee?" "Yes, please!" That's not a recipe for romance, my friends - that's more like a recipe for awkward encounters!

So, let's dish out some real-world advice, straight from the love kitchen. Instead of rushing in like a bull in a china shop, let's take it slow and steady, like a cozy Sunday brunch.

If you fancy someone, sprinkle a little flirtation into the mix – it's like adding a dash of spice to your recipe for romance. Build a genuine connection, like stirring the ingredients together until they blend perfectly. Don't worry, we'll cover flirting and connection in the next chapter.

And remember, my dear love connoisseurs, premature displays of affection can be like tossing a pot of boiling water into the mix – it might look impressive, but it's not the best move. Let those emotions simmer, and allow the flavors of love to develop naturally.

Premature declarations may cause a communication meltdown – it's like trying to speak a foreign language without any practice! Effective communication needs time and trust to marinate into something meaningful.

Now, don't get me wrong - movies are like the dessert of life, sweet and indulgent. But real-life love is more like a hearty main course – it takes time, effort, and patience to prepare something truly delicious.

So, my fellow love chefs, let's savor the journey and leave the movie clichés on the big screen where they belong. By blending flirting and connection, we'll create a love story that's uniquely ours – a real-life romance worth celebrating!

👎 Being Overly Nice

Ah, the age-old saying, "Nice guys finish last" – like a marathon for kindness, huh? But hold your good deeds, my fellow nice guys, because being overly nice might not always get you that winner's trophy in the dating game!

Picture this: you're kind, considerate, and polite – like a gentleman from a 19th-century romance novel. But sometimes, being too nice can lead to more plot twists than a soap opera!

Now, I don't want you to misunderstand me – being nice is like the icing on the cake of life. But sometimes, you might find yourself stuck in a sweet, sticky situation like a cupcake in a bakery display.

Why? Well, those excessively nice vibes might come off like a "Yes Man" who's always nodding along. And trust me, my friends, confidence is the secret sauce that spices up the dating recipe!

And speaking of recipes, you don't want to be like a one-item menu in the restaurant of love. Being taken for granted can feel like eating the same meal every day – eventually, you'll want something new on the menu!

Setting boundaries is like seasoning in a relationship – it adds just the right amount of spice! But too much "nice" might leave you bland, like an unseasoned dish.

Now, let's talk about that allure of mystery – it's like a treasure hunt in the dating world. Being too transparent might be like giving away the map too soon – the thrill of the chase disappears!

And don't be mistaken for a ride in the friend-zone rollercoaster! It's like buying a ticket for a thrilling romance ride, but ending up on the kiddie train instead.

So, my kind-hearted comrades, let's sprinkle some assertiveness into the mix. Be like a pizza with all the right toppings – confident, respectful, and able to speak your mind!

Remember, it's like a dance of flavors – being nice is just one step. The real magic happens when you mix kindness with authenticity, assertiveness, and clear communication.

So, let's be the complete dish – the kind of partner that's both sweet and spicy! Strike that balance, and you'll find yourself savoring a love that's worth every bite!

👎 Lying

The land of lies – a treacherous territory where trust goes to die. And my dear friends, let me tell you, lying to women is like trying to build a sandcastle in a tsunami – It's bound to wash away all chances of a successful relationship!

Picture this: you're starting to connect with a lovely lady, but instead of being true to yourself, you whip out a disguise like a secret agent on a mission. But here's the catch – once the mask is off, the trust will be too!

So, let's talk about the deadly lies that can turn your love story into a Shakespearean tragedy:

First up, **false identity** – like a chameleon changing colors, pretending to be someone you're not will leave you caught in a web of deception.

Next, **relationship status shenanigans** – telling half-truths about your love life is like dancing on a landmine, ready to explode any moment!

And who can forget about the **bragging blunders** – like a fisherman with a tall tale, exaggerating your achievements will reel them in, but only to let them slip away!

Pretending to like the same hobbies? Now, that's a recipe for disaster – it's like a vegan at a meat festival, just waiting to be caught red-handed!

Hiding past relationships is like burying secrets in the love garden – sooner or later, those skeletons will start haunting the relationship.

Financial misrepresentation? Oh, you've got to be kidding! That's like showing up at a yacht party on a paddleboat!

And let's not forget about the **intentions puzzle** – saying you want a long-term relationship when you're only after a fling is like setting a relationship time bomb.

Oh, and **age or appearance lies?** Trust me, my friends, that's like Photoshopping your dating profile – sooner or later, they'll see the real picture!

So, let's raise our honesty flags high and sail the seas of trust! In the early stages of a relationship, it's like planting the seeds of truth – with care and nurture – a genuine and healthy love will bloom!

Remember, my fellow love sailors, honesty is the North Star that guides us to a love that's real, deep, and built on trust. So, let's navigate these waters with integrity and sail toward a love that lasts a lifetime!

👎 Being Too Apologetic

The art of apologizing – a dance between humility and self-assurance. But let's face it, my friends, saying sorry for every little thing is like sprinkling confetti on a rainy day – it just doesn't make sense!

Picture this: you accidentally brush against someone's shoulder, and before you know it, you're saying sorry like you're in a never-ending apology marathon! It's like the sorry train has left the station, and you're the conductor!

Now, apologies are like a safety net in a trapeze act; they catch us when we stumble. But overusing sorry is like pouring ketchup on a perfectly good dish – it ruins the flavor!

Instead, be like a confident acrobat on the tightrope of life – apologize when it truly matters. When you mess up, show genuine remorse and accountability, like a magician revealing their secret!

Remember, my friends, a sincere apology is like a rare gem – it's precious and meaningful. But if you toss apologies around like confetti, it's like losing that sparkle!

So, let's find that sweet spot between humility and self-assurance – apologize when it counts, and stand firm when you've done nothing wrong. It's like the graceful dance of a peacock – striking the perfect balance!

Now go forth, my friends, and let your apologies be like gold – valuable and cherished, not like confetti – flying around without a purpose!

👎 Constantly Asking Permission to do Things

The dance of decision-making in relationships – a waltz of respect and consideration. But beware, my friends, for seeking permission for every little thing can turn that waltz into a stumbling tango of indecisiveness!

Picture this: you're walking on eggshells, like a clumsy ballerina tiptoeing around. "Can I order this? Is it okay if I get that?" – it's like trying to navigate a minefield of decisions!

Now, allow me to explain – being considerate is like the seasoning of love, adding that extra flavor to the relationship. But constantly asking for permission is like overdosing on the salt - it ruins the dish!

So, let's find that sweet spot between collaboration and autonomy – like a perfect recipe that satisfies both partners' appetites. Communication is the secret ingredient that binds it all together!

Now, let's dive into some menu examples to see the difference between being considerate and seeking permission:

First up, ordering food – it's like a menu of options, but constantly asking, "Can I order this? Can I get that?" is like being stuck in a restaurant limbo!

Instead, show some flair and confidently say, "I'm thinking of getting the pasta. What about you?" – It's like adding some spice to the dinner table conversation!

Next, planning a date – like a director, you want to impress your leading lady. But constantly asking, "Is it all right if we go to the movies? Would you mind if we grab dinner afterward?" – It's like directing a rom-com with too many plot twists!

Show some initiative, my friends, and suggest a plan, "I thought it would be fun to catch a movie and have dinner afterward. What do you think?" – it's like giving her a sneak peek into your date vision!

Now, personal space – like a respectful gentleman, you want to be close, but constantly asking, "Can I sit next to you? Can I hold your hand?" – it's like navigating a touchy-feely maze!

Ah, the delicate dance of intimate moves – where actions speak louder than words! But let me tell you, my dear friends, when it comes to kissing, you don't need an instruction manual or a permission slip!

Imagine this scenario: you're leaning in for that magical moment, heart pounding like a bass drum. But wait, you stop and ask, "Can I kiss you now?" It's like putting the brakes on a romantic rollercoaster!

Now, just to be clear – consent is like the foundation of any dance, and it's crucial to be attentive to your partner's cues. But asking for permission to kiss is like reading a choreography script at a ballroom dance – it kills the romance!

Instead, pay attention to her body language and verbal cues – it's like reading the rhythm of the music on the dance floor. If you sense she's interested and comfortable, go for it! Let the chemistry guide your moves!

Remember, my friends, a kiss is like the crescendo of a beautiful symphony of emotions. When it's the right moment, you'll feel it in your heart – no words needed, just the silent language of love!

So, let's ditch the constant permission-seeking and embrace the balance of consideration and confidence. Like a symphony of trust and respect, open communication will be the melody that keeps your relationship dancing in harmony!

👎 Heavy Conversations

Heavy conversations – like carrying a suitcase full of bricks on a first date. Not the best idea, my friends, unless you want to leave your date feeling like they've been through a marathon!

Picture this: you're at a lovely dinner, enjoying a delicious meal, and suddenly, you dive into the depths of past traumas and family dramas. It's like going from a tasty appetizer to a full-on emotional feast!

Now, sharing deeper feelings and experiences is like adding spice to a relationship stew, but timing is everything! You wouldn't want to serve dessert before the main course, right?

So, instead of dropping heavy topics like anvils, let's be savvy conversationalists! Like a chef, we'll introduce the right ingredients at the perfect moment to create a delightful connection soufflé!

First, focus on the light and fun – talk about hobbies, interests, and the wacky things that make you both laugh! It's like sprinkling humor all over your conversations!

Then, as trust and comfort grow like a well-tended garden, you can start sprinkling in those deeper topics. It's like adding a dash of depth to your delightful dish!

Remember, my friends, relationships are like slow-cooked masterpieces – they take time and patience. So, let's simmer in the fun and joy before serving up the emotional entrees!

Now go forth, my savvy daters, and build connections that are light, fun, and meaningful – like a balanced meal that leaves everyone satisfied and wanting more! Bon appétit!

👎 Talking About Past Relationships

The dreaded past relationship talk – a tightrope walk between sharing and oversharing. Let's navigate this conversation like acrobats, my friends, with grace to lead the way!

Picture this: you're on a date, and suddenly the conversation turns into a marathon of ex-talk! It's like watching a soap opera with way too many seasons – you just can't keep up!

Now, don't get me wrong – discussing past experiences is like flipping through the pages of a well-worn book. But we don't want to read the entire novel on the first date, right?

So, instead of reciting the ex-files like a detective novel, let's add some humor to lighten the mood! It's like throwing a pinch of laughter into the mix, making it more digestible!

First, let's avoid the comparison game like a pro – nobody wants to feel like they're in a competition! It's like comparing apples and oranges, my friends, and we all know fruit salads are much tastier!

Next, let's steer clear of relationship drama like avoiding rush hour traffic! Drama-free zones are our destination, and we'll take the express lane to happiness!

Now, here's the secret sauce: keep the focus on the present and future like a fortune teller predicting love and joy! It's like reading the stars and seeing a bright and beautiful journey ahead!

Remember, my savvy daters, past relationships are like stepping stones that led us to this moment. So, let's learn from them, but not dwell on them! We're writing a new chapter together!

Now go forth with humor, zest, and a sprinkle of present-moment magic. Let's create connections that are free of baggage and full of joy – like a vacation from ex-talk! Bon voyage!

👎 Chasing Women

The timeless pursuit of someone you fancy. It's like being on a quest for buried treasure – exciting, nerve-wracking, and sometimes, you might stumble upon a pirate's curse! But fear not, my fellow adventurers, for I shall guide you through this treacherous terrain with a touch of tact and a map to navigate the twists and turns of pursuing someone special!

Imagine this: you're on a mission to win her heart, but you don't want to turn into a human-homing missile! We want her heart, not a lock-on target!

First things first – mutual interest is like a dance floor, my savvy daters. You need both partners to groove together for a smooth and delightful experience!

Now, let's avoid overwhelming her with attention like a swarm of buzzing bees – we're going for charm, not a beekeeping convention!

And beware of the "desperate desperado" trap! We don't want to chase her like a dog chasing its tail – it's all about balance, folks!

Mystery and intrigue are like spices in the recipe of romance. We want to keep her guessing, not giving away the ending like a movie spoiler!

Remember, respecting boundaries is like finding the right temperature for your morning coffee – too hot, and it burns; too cold, and it's just not right!

Now, let's replace chasing with genuine connection like trading in a clunky old car for a sleek and shiny new one! Smooth and comfortable!

Instead of constant pursuit, let's engage in meaningful conversations and shared activities – it's like cooking up a recipe for love together!

And here's the secret ingredient: give her the space to develop her feelings like a fine wine that gets better with time!

So, my fellow pursuers, let's embrace tact, respect, and genuine interest in this dance of romance. Remember, it's not about the chase; it's about the connection! Happy dating, everyone!

🖓 Being Overly Possessive or Controlling

Let me share a little secret with you. Being overly possessive or controlling is like trying to put a leash on a unicorn – it just ain't gonna work! You see, women are like majestic creatures of the wild, with minds of their own and a spirit that can't be tamed.

Imagine this: you're on a first date, and she's looking all cute and confident like a fierce lioness strutting her stuff. But then, you start acting like a paranoid meerkat, constantly checking her phone, asking where she's going, and who she's talking to. Trust me, it's not a good look. You might as well break out a neon sign that says, 'Warning: Stage-5 Clinger!'

Now, picture this: you've planned a fun outing together, but you turn into a GPS tracker, monitoring her every move like a detective on a top-secret mission. "Babe, why'd you take that left turn? I thought we were going right!" She playfully rolls her eyes, giving you a look like a sassy flamingo, and teases, "Relax, Mr. GPS, a little detour won't hurt!" You can't help but laugh at your overly cautious self. Nobody wants a relationship with a walking, talking navigation system. Remember, it's all about embracing the journey together and not getting lost in the details.

Let's not forget the "one-size-fits-all" mentality. Trying to mold her into your ideal version of a girlfriend is like trying to force a giraffe into ballet shoes. It's just not gonna happen, folks. Women are unique and wonderful creatures with their quirks and passions. Embrace that, and you'll have a much better time.

So, gentlemen, here's the moral of the story: be confident in yourself, trust your partner, and let her roam free like the amazing wild creature she is. Trying to control her will only lead to disaster. Embrace the adventure, and who knows, you might just find yourself dancing with that enchanting unicorn under the moonlight!

👎 Demanding Exclusivity Too Early

In the quirky world of dating and relationships, mastering the fine art of balance between expressing your desires and respecting your partner's boundaries can feel like doing the hokey-pokey blind-folded. When it comes to exclusivity, it's like walking a tightrope between two tall buildings – tricky, precarious, and not for the faint of heart. Pushing for exclusivity too soon can be like trying to fit a square peg into a round hole – awkward and bound to backfire. So, let's unravel why demanding exclusivity prematurely might leave you with one foot out the door, and how a dash of patience and open communication can lead to a beautiful commitment:

❑ **Pressure and Control:** Ever tried playing peekaboo with a kitten? Demanding exclusivity too early can feel like that – making the woman want to hide and disappear until the coast is clear. Nobody likes feeling backed into a corner.

❑ **Lack of Trust:** Trust is like a delicate teacup; one wrong move, and it shatters. Insisting on exclusivity before trust has a chance to brew can leave the woman wondering, "Is this person too clingy like that piece of gum stuck to my shoe?"

❑ **Rushing the Relationship:** Love is like a slow-cooked stew; it needs time to simmer and blend the flavors. Demanding exclusivity too soon is like microwaving the stew – it won't taste right, and you'll get burnt.

❑ **Fear of Being Trapped:** Imagine trying to catch a butterfly with a fishnet – it just won't happen. Demanding exclusivity can make the woman feel like she's caught in a net and can't flutter freely.

❑ **Independence and Autonomy:** Everyone needs their personal space, like a snail carrying its cozy shell. Demanding exclusivity too early can feel like you're encroaching on her space and making her retreat into her shell.

❑ **Emotional Readiness:** Each heart has its own rhythm, like a funky dance party. Demanding exclusivity before the music even starts can leave the woman thinking, "Hold up, I need to feel the beat first!"

❏ **Unresolved Concerns:** Relationships are like a jigsaw puzzle; you need all the pieces to fit together. Demanding exclusivity might skip the puzzle-solving and jump straight to gluing the pieces, but that won't make the picture complete.

Instead of bumbling like a bear in a beehive, let the connection bloom naturally like a beautiful garden. Express your feelings and intentions honestly, but don't bulldoze over her boundaries. Exclusivity is like a warm blanket; you'll both cozy up to it when the time is right. It's like a waltz – taking the right steps together, gracefully and in harmony. So, put on your dancing shoes and enjoy the dance of love!

👎 Taking Things Too Seriously

Oh, commitment and responsibility are like the superheroes of the dating world, but hey, let's not take things so seriously right from the get-go! Here's why being a little too intense can make the whole interaction feel like a business meeting instead of a romantic rendezvous:

❏ **Limited Relaxation:** This creates an environment that lacks relaxation and inhibits the woman from feeling at ease during the conversation.

❏ **High Pressure:** This can make the woman feel overwhelmed and under pressure to meet serious expectations early on.

❏ **Lack of Playfulness:** The absence of light-heartedness and humor may result in a lack of enjoyable, memorable moments.

❏ **Diminished Spontaneity:** Over-seriousness might hinder

the flow of natural, spontaneous conversation and interactions.

☐ **Difficulty Connecting:** It becomes harder for the woman to establish a genuine emotional connection if everything is treated with excessive seriousness.

☐ **Formal Atmosphere:** The interaction may feel overly formal and less inviting for the woman to express herself freely.

☐ **Fear of Mistakes:** This creates an atmosphere where the woman might be afraid of making mistakes, leading to self-censorship.

☐ **Uncomfortable Environment:** Taking things too seriously can make the woman feel uncomfortable and cautious in her responses.

☐ **Limited Emotional Range:** Diminishes the opportunity to showcase different emotions, as the focus remains on being serious.

☐ **Difficulty Reading the Woman's Reactions:** Over-seriousness might make it harder to gauge the woman's true feelings and reactions.

Mind that this is just the first date, not a boardroom meeting! So, let's sprinkle in some laughter, ease up on the intense vibes, and find that sweet spot where we can be serious and playful at the same time. It's all about striking the perfect balance and creating an atmosphere where we can be our authentic selves while having a great time together. Let's turn this into a memorable and enjoyable experience for both of us!

👎 Being Too Logical

Well, my mighty logician, let me tickle your funny bone with a tale of romance and reason gone awry! Picture this: you, the Captain of Logic, steering the ship of seduction with precision and meticulousness.

In the realm of love, imagine your brain as a high-speed computer, processing every interaction like a boss. "Error, error! Too much logic!" cries your heart from the depths of emotion.

As you lock eyes with a potential romantic interest, your inner geek takes over. "Calculating optimal flirting technique. Initiating witty banter in 3... 2... 1..." But alas, the moment slips away like a mischievous rascal, leaving you in a state of logical befuddlement.

When she shares a heartwarming story, your brain races to analyze its authenticity. "Probability of truth: 82.3%. Emotional connection status: pending."

As you attempt to open a conversation, your logical self takes control. "Comparing icebreaker options. Scanning for optimal choice... Error! Icebreaker.exe not found."

Oh, dear Captain, beware of the danger of overthinking! Love is not a mathematical equation to be solved, but a delightful rollercoaster of emotions.

Imagine serenading her with a perfectly timed song, only to hear a robotic voice singing "Love algorithms activated. Melody output: check."

But fear not, valiant logician! Strike a balance between reason and romance. Remember, sometimes the best outcomes come from a little chaos and spontaneity.

So, my dear Captain of Logic, let your charming geek shine through. Let go of the need for flawless precision and embrace the delightful messiness of love.

And when in doubt, simply follow your heart's hilarious error messages. "Warning: butterflies in stomach detected. Emotion overload. Proceed with caution... or not!"

Happy navigating, oh logical adventurer, through the whimsical seas of seduction!

👎 Poor Body Language

The unspoken language of body gestures and postures awaits our exploration. After all, who knew our bodies could say so much without uttering a single word? Here are some poor body language examples and some valuable tips to rock the nonverbal communication game and create meaningful connections:

○ **Avoiding Eye Contact:** If you stare at the floor, she might think you're searching for hidden treasure. Keep those eyes up and engage in some good ol' eye contact, mate!

○ **Crossed Arms:** Arms crossed like a fortress? Are you preparing for a battle of wits? Show some openness and let those arms relax a bit!

○ **Closed-Off Posture:** Hunching like you're auditioning for "The Quasimodo Chronicles"?[1] Stand tall, my friend, and show some confidence!

○ **Fidgeting or Nervous Movements:** Shake, shake, shake! Oops, not the dance floor. Relax, take a deep breath, and save the dance moves for later.

○ **Standing Too Close:** Remember, personal space is like your secret superhero lair – let her have hers!

○ **Leaning Away:** Leaning back like you're avoiding a pie in the face? Lean in, my friend, and show you're all ears (and not afraid of pies).

○ **Checking Phone Constantly:** Hold on, is your phone more captivating than your date? Put that phone away and give her your undivided attention!

○ **Lack of Smiling:** Who forgot to put on their smile today? Flash those pearly whites and let happiness be contagious!

○ **Crossing Legs:** Crossing your legs can send a message of over-the-top self-control, which is basically like saying, "I'm

---

[1] "The Quasimodo Chronicles" was used metaphorically to humorously refer to a closed-off posture, similar to how the character Quasimodo is often depicted in Victor Hugo's novel "The Hunchback of Notre Dame." Quasimodo is known for his hunched posture, and the term was used to emphasize the importance of standing tall and showing confidence instead of displaying closed-off body language.

not sure about this." Trust me, it's not a great fashion state-ment. So, let's avoid the insecurity signals and keep the vibe comfortable!

◌ **Restless Movements:** Shifting weight like you're on a high-speed train? Stay grounded and be present in the moment.

Good body language is like a magic potion that exudes confi-dence, openness, and approachability. Keep those eyes twinkling, arms relaxed, and give her the space to feel comfortable. Nod along with the conversation, but don't turn it into a bobblehead show!

A natural way to develop good body language, without resorting to complex explanations of posture (which can be confusing and not suitable for everyone), is by engaging in regular physical activity. Participating in any form of consistent physical activity, whether it's working out, jogging, swimming, or hiking, can naturally enhance your physical fitness and posture. Furthermore, each outdoor adventure or gym session provides an additional opportunity to meet interesting people, including that intriguing woman you've been dreaming about.

Other activities that naturally bring about positive changes in your body language include dance classes, group exercise classes, yoga, pilates, and martial arts. In addition to posture correction, these activities offer various benefits, such as stress relief, fostering positive mindsets, and creating opportunities to meet women.

While the turn-offs we've explored in this section might hit the mark with some lovely ladies, keep in mind that each person is a unique puzzle with their own preferences and quirks. What one gal finds as charming as a one-eyed pirate, another might find as ap-pealing as a basket of puppies!

And now, my intrepid daters, get ready for the next thrilling chapter where we'll dive headfirst into the captivating art of flirting and building genuine connections that will set the stage for a ro-mance like no other. See ya there!

Chapter 2
MASTERING ENGAGING CHATS

Up until now, we've only scratched the tip of the iceberg, delving into the importance of self-awareness and knowing what we desire in a relationship, leading us to attract the right partner. Additionally, we've explored the intriguing factors that influence women's choices when it comes to choosing a partner. But our journey doesn't end there; we still have some more ground to cover, particularly when it comes to capturing a woman's heart.

As promised, in this chapter, we will discuss how to spice up conversations with women using a bit of flirting to make our romantic intentions clear and how to create connections to keep their interest in you alive.

So, in the following sections, we'll explore the magic of flirting, the skill of making engaging small talk, and the art of building meaningful connections. By mastering these aspects, you'll be well on your way to capturing and maintaining the interest of the women you desire.

1. Verbal Sparks: The Flirt's Toolkit

Flirting entails using witty lines that make you appear sweet and spicy simultaneously, setting the tone for playful interactions and paving the way for meaningful connections and potential relationships. As I like to say, flirting is the foreplay before meaningful conversations, inviting her on a date, or making intimate moves.

Before we dive into flirty remarks and examples of how conversations might flow with their incorporation, it's essential to remember that flirting should be introduced right from the start of an interaction. Let me explain why this is crucial:

When you have your first encounter with a woman you're interested in, you want to create certain expectations. You need her to see you as a potential partner, not just a casual acquaintance. Timing plays a vital role too. If you initially engage in discussions that strictly revolve around serious or generic topics and then abruptly shift to flirting, she will be surprised because she was not aware of this side of you, and that's not the kind of surprise you want to give her. To avoid this, it's important to introduce flirting from the very first exchange of words. Yes, she might be caught off guard in the beginning, but that is the right time to do so. Afterward, you can have conversations about everyday matters like the weather, work, and gossip, but don't forget to sprinkle them from time to time with a touch of flirtation.

🙂 Flirty Starters

Flirty starters are fantastic tools to catch a woman's attention and kick-start a playful conversation when she's introduced to you. It helps avoid the awkwardness of an interview-style interaction or early silence. For each starter, I'll provide a dialog example to give you an idea of how your conversation could flow. So, let's explore some flirty starters together!

Example #1:

Girl: "Nice to meet you!"
Guy: *"Of course, you are, as I always say, if you meet me, you have an awesome day!"*

🗨 **Conversation:**

Setting: A social gathering where a man named Alex is introduced to a woman named Rachel.

Friend: (Introducing Rachel to Alex) "Hey Alex, I want you to meet my friend Rachel. She's such a fun person to be around."
Alex: (Smiling) "Hi Rachel, it's a pleasure to meet you."
Rachel: "Nice to meet you too, Alex."
Alex: (Playfully) "Of course, you are, as I always say, if you meet me, you have an awesome day!"
Rachel: (Laughing) "Well, I must say, that's a confidence booster. You really know how to make an entrance!"
Alex: "Can't help it; it's my party trick. I believe in spreading positive vibes wherever I go."
Rachel: "That's a great party trick to have. Positive energy is contagious!"
Alex: "Absolutely! So, what brings you to this fantastic party tonight?"
Rachel: "Just looking for a good time and meeting new people. And I guess I've already succeeded in the latter!"
Alex: "Mission accomplished then! You've met a funny guy and a promise of an awesome day."
Rachel: "A Day that started with this party and meeting you? It's already off to a great start."
Alex: "Well, I'm flattered! But let's keep the night going and make it even more memorable."

(They both share a laugh and continue chatting, enjoying each other's company throughout the party.)

Note: In this playful conversation, Alex uses a light-hearted and humorous response to Rachel's "Nice to meet you." He confidently shares a playful line, and Rachel responds with humor and positivity, creating a fun atmosphere. Playful banter like this can be a great way to break the ice and form a connection with someone in almost any setting, not necessarily at a social event.

Example #2:

Guy: *"What is your favorite cuisine?"*
Girl: [Response]
Guy: *"Great! Tomorrow when we go on our second date, I'll take you to an* [her response] *restaurant."*

💬 **Conversation:**

Setting: An office breakroom with colleagues gathered for introductions.

Colleague: (Introducing the woman, Shelby, to the guy, Mark) "Hey Mark, I want you to meet our newest team member, Shelby. She's joining us as a marketing specialist."
Mark: (Smiling and extending his hand) "Hi Shelby, welcome aboard! It's great to have you on the team. By the way, what is your favorite cuisine?"
Shelby: (Shaking Mark's hand) "Thank you, Mark! Nice to meet you too. I'm a big fan of Italian cuisine – pasta and pizza are my weaknesses."
Mark: "Great! Tomorrow when we go on our second date, I'll take you to an Italian restaurant."
Shelby: (Laughing) "Oh, second date already, huh? You move

fast! But I appreciate the restaurant choice."

Mark: (Smirking) "Well, time flies in the office, and I can't wait to get to know you better outside of work."

Shelby: "Flattery will get you everywhere, won't it? Alright, Italian it is for our imaginary second date."

Mark: "Imaginary or not, I'm looking forward to it. We'll have a pizza-filled time!"

Colleague: (Teasingly) "Looks like you two are already planning a future together."

Mark: "Hey, why wait? Life is short, and good company and good food make it all the better."

Shelby: "True, can't argue with that logic! I'm always up for good food and good company."

Mark: "Then we have a deal! It's a date, imaginary or not."

Shelby: "Deal! Looking forward to our 'imaginary' Italian adventure."

(They all share a laugh as they continue chatting and getting to know each other in the office breakroom.)

Note: In this example, Mark uses a light-hearted and playful line to initiate a conversation with Shelby, and they share a humorous exchange about an "imaginary" second date. By starting this way, he displays his playful nature, paving the way for more flirty remarks, and if a connection is made, a discussion about an actual date will naturally occur.

Example #3:

"What's the best thing a guy can say to start flirting with a girl he just met?"

🗨 **Conversation:**

Setting: A cozy and elegant dinner party at a friend's beautiful home, complete with dimmed lights, soft background music, and a mix of intimate conversations happening throughout the room.

Friend: "Hey Tom, I want you to meet my friend Emma. Emma, this is Tom."

Emma: "Hi Tom, nice to meet you!"

Tom: "Hi Emma, pleasure to meet you too! So, I've got a bit of a random question for you. What's the best thing a guy can say to start flirting with a girl he just met?"

Emma (smiling): "Oh, really? Are you asking for a friend, or is this a personal inquiry?"

Tom (playfully): "Haha, let's just say I like to be prepared for any situation."

Emma: "Well, I think a genuine compliment is always a good start. Something that shows you noticed something about her that goes beyond just looks."

Tom: "That's a great piece of advice. I'll have to keep that in mind. By the way, I must say, you have a fantastic sense of style. That dress looks stunning on you."

Emma (blushing): "Thank you, Tom. You're not so bad yourself. I can see you've got a great sense of humor."

Tom: "Oh, I try my best. So, Emma, tell me something interesting about yourself. What's your hidden talent or a quirky hobby?"

Emma: "Hmm, well, I can do a pretty convincing dolphin impression. But I'll have to show you sometime when the party isn't too crowded."

Tom: "I'll definitely hold you to that. I'm intrigued now!"

(And the conversation continues, with both Tom and Emma engaging in light-hearted banter and getting to know each other better throughout the evening, amidst the warm ambiance of the dinner party.)

Note: In this example, Tom starts a playful conversation by asking Emma a quirky question, but Emma responds with grace and humor. Tom continued flirting by skillfully complimenting Emma's style and exchanging stories about hidden talents.

Example #4:

"I hope you won't take it personally if I'm not flirting with you right away. First, I must present you to my parents."

🗫 **Conversation:**

Setting: A team-building event organized by a company. The event is held in a vibrant venue with team-building activities, games, and opportunities for socializing. Robert and Mia connect during a moment of introductions, leading to their delightful exchange of playful remarks.

> **Robert:** (with a mischievous smile) "Ah, Mia, a pleasure to meet you! I hope you won't take it personally if I'm not flirting with you right away. First, I must present you to my parents."
> **Mia:** (laughs) "Well, Robert, that's quite a unique approach to meeting someone! I promise not to take it personally. But, are you always this cautious with new acquaintances?"
> **Robert:** (playfully) "Only when they have a name as enchanting as yours, Mia. You see, I have a reputation to uphold with my parents. They raised me to have impeccable taste in the people I bring into their lives."
> **Mia:** (teasingly) "I'm flattered by your high standards! I must admit, my name has never been an entry requirement before. But I'll gladly pass the parent test with flying colors."
> **Robert:** (grinning) "Excellent! Just a fair warning, though my parents have a tendency to spoil my friends with excessive des-

serts, so you better be prepared for some serious sweet indulgence."

Mia: (enthusiastically) "Oh, I can handle any dessert challenge they throw at me! I have a sweet tooth that's ready for the ultimate test. Consider me your newest dessert partner in crime!"

Note: The conversation between Robert and Mia is playful and full of banter. Robert's lighthearted comment sets the tone for their friendly exchange. Both participants engage in humorous remarks, creating an enjoyable and relaxed atmosphere. As they continue to chat, they build rapport and share a fun connection during the team-building event.

Example #5:

"Is there a lighthouse nearby, or is it just your smile that lights up the whole room?"

🗩 Conversation:

Setting: A lively party with music and people socializing.

Friend: (Introducing the woman, Sarah, to the guy, Rick) "Hey Rick, I want you to meet my friend Sarah. She's an amazing person, and I think you two will get along great!"

Rick: (Smiling) "Hi Sarah, it's a pleasure to meet you. So, is there a lighthouse nearby, or is it just your smile that lights up the whole room?"

Sarah: (Blushing and laughing) "Wow, that's quite the line! I'll admit, you caught me off guard with that one. I guess I'll take it as a compliment."

Rick: (Grinning) "Absolutely! There might not be a lighthouse, but your smile does have a way of brightening up the party."

Sarah: "You're quite the charmer, Rick. I appreciate the creative approach."

Rick: "Thank you! It's all in good fun. So, how do you like the party so far?"

Sarah: "It's great! The music is fantastic, and the atmosphere is so lively. It's my kind of party."

Rick: "I'm glad you're enjoying it. Let's make it even better by having a great time together."

Sarah: "I'm up for that! By the way, did you come up with that lighthouse line all on your own?"

Rick: (Laughing) "Guilty as charged! I have a friend who's convinced he's a stand-up comedian, and he's always trying to teach me his tricks."

Sarah: "Well, it seems like his tricks are working. That line definitely got my attention."

Rick: "Mission accomplished, then! I must say, your friend wasn't wrong about us getting along great."

Sarah: "I agree! I have a feeling this party just got a whole lot more interesting."

Rick: "It's all thanks to your dazzling smile. Let's make this a party to remember."

(They both continue chatting and laughing, hitting it off as they enjoy each other's company at the party.)

Note: In a party setting, humor and friendly banter are a fun way to break the ice and create a positive connection between people. The key is to keep the humor light, genuine, and appropriate for the situation. In this example, Rick uses a playful line to start the conversation with Sarah, and they engage in an enjoyable interaction at the party.

Example #6:

Guy: **"Have you ever wondered what a perfect crime should**

look like?"
Girl: [Response]
Guy: **"Well, I'll steal your heart, and you can steal mine. Sorry, I can't help myself; cheesy pickup lines are my guilty pleasure."**

💬 Conversation:

Setting: A vibrant nightclub with pulsing music, colorful lights, and people dancing and laughing all around. Ava is introduced to Eddy by a mutual friend.

Friend: "Eddy this is Ava. Ava this is Eddy."
Ava: "Nice to meet you, Eddy."
Eddy: "Pleasure's all mine, Ava. So, have you ever wondered what a perfect crime should look like?"
Ava: (chuckles) "Well, I guess I never thought about it. What do you have in mind?"
Eddy: "Oh, nothing too sinister. But here's my plan: I'll steal your heart, and you can steal mine."
Ava: (laughs) "Stealing hearts, huh? That's quite an ambitious crime! Though not so original."
Eddy: (grinning) "Guilty as charged! I can't help myself; cheesy pickup lines are my weakness."
Ava: "Well, you're not alone there. They're oddly endearing."
Eddy: (playfully) "See, we're already partners in crime!"
Ava: "I guess we are! So, what other heists are you planning tonight?"
Eddy: "Hmm, how about we steal the spotlight on the dance floor?"
Ava: "Sounds like a plan! Let's show them our moves."

Note: In this playful conversation, Eddy starts with a cheesy pickup line to break the ice and create a fun atmosphere. The "perfect crime" line acts as an attention-grabber, leading to a witty exchange between Eddy and Ava about "stealing hearts." Their playful banter and shared enjoyment of cheesy pickup lines allowed them to connect on a lighthearted level, setting the stage for an enjoyable night of laughter, dancing, and forming a genuine connection amidst the energetic nightclub setting.

Example #7:

"Well, I hope you know CPR 'cause you make my heart bit faster than a bullet train!"

🗩 Conversation:

Setting: John and Gina are introduced to each other by a mutual friend at a social event, a lively cocktail party with music and laughter in the background.

John: (with a playful grin) "Hi Gina, I hope you know CPR 'cause you make my heart beat faster than a bullet train!"
Gina: (laughs) "Oh, that's a new one! But lucky for you, I've got my CPR certification just in case. Safety first, right?"
John: (smiling) "Safety and charm, a winning combination. So, how did you end up at this event?"
Gina: (casually) "Oh, I heard about this gathering through a friend, and thought it might be a fun way to spend the evening. And I must say, meeting someone with bullet train speed heartbeats was not on my radar."
John: (teasingly) "Serendipity works in mysterious ways! Speaking of mysteries, tell me something fascinating about yourself."
Gina: (playfully) "Well, did you know I can name all the U.S. presidents in chronological order? Comes in handy during trivia nights, I promise."

John: (impressed) "The ultimate presidential knowledge, I'm impressed! But let's save the trivia challenge for another time. For now, how about we enjoy this fantastic event together?"
Gina: (enthusiastically) "I'm all in! Lead the way, Mr. Bullet Train Heartbeat."

Note: The conversation unfolds with a playful banter that sounds ripped straight from the heart of the internet but works wonders in certain situations. As they share tidbits about their interests and talents, they discover common ground and enjoy each other's company. The playful and relaxed atmosphere at the party encourages them to continue the conversation and explore more about each other.

Example #8: Mixed Banters

Version #1

Guy: ***"Do you know what they say about*** [something about her look] ***girls?"*** (e.g., hair or outfit)
Girl: [response]
Guy: ***"They are good flirts."***
        [.....................................]
Guy: **"You know what else they say?"**
Girl: [response]
Guy: ***"They are also good dancers. Any chance I can convince you to show me some moves later?"***
        [.....................................]
        "…. If you meet me, you have an awesome day." (a line that was mentioned earlier in this section.)

        "So, when are you planning to ask me out?" (This can be used after a few rounds of playful banters.)

🗨 Conversation:

Setting: A lively bar with music and people enjoying their drinks. Jenny is introduced to Dan by a mutual friend.

Friend: (Introducing Jenny to Dan) "Dan, meet Jenny. Jenny, meet Dan."

Dan: (Smiling) "Hi Jenny, it's great to meet you. Nice hair, by the way. You know what they said about brunet girls..."

Jenny: (Curious) "Oh, what do they say about brunet girls?"

Dan: "They are good flirts."

Jenny: (Playfully) "Oh, really? I guess I'll have to live up to the reputation then."

Dan: "The bar is set high, but I have a feeling you'll surpass it."

Jenny: "Well, we'll see about that!"

Dan: "You know what else they say?"

Jenny: "Amaze me!"

Dan: "They are also good dancers. Any chance I can convince you to show me some moves later?"

Jenny: "Hmm, it depends. Can you keep up?"

Dan: "I might need some practice, but I promise not to step on your toes."

Jenny: (Laughing) "Deal! I'll be your dance instructor for the night."

Dan: "I couldn't ask for a better teacher."

Jenny: "Flattery will get you everywhere, won't it?"

Dan: "Well, they do say if you meet me, you have an awesome day."

Jenny: (Smirking) "You're quite confident, aren't you?"

Dan: "Confidence is key, but I can back it up with a great sense of humor."

Jenny: "I'll be the judge of that!"

Dan: "Fair enough. So, when are you planning to ask me out for that dance session?"

Jenny: (Laughing) "Oh, so now you're assuming I'll be the one asking you out?"

Dan: "Well, they also say 'fortune favors the bold,' and I'm feeling pretty bold right now."

Jenny: "Bold it is then! I'll let you know when I'm ready to see those dance moves."

Dan: "I'll be eagerly waiting for that invitation."

(They both share a laugh, continuing their playful and engaging conversation throughout the evening at the bar, building a connection through their banter and shared interests.)

Note: In this playful conversation, Dan starts with a light-hearted remark about Jenny's hair, leading into friendly banter about brunet girls being good flirts. The conversation naturally progresses into discussing a hypothetical dance session. The playful exchange creates a fun and engaging atmosphere between them, laying the groundwork for potential future interaction.

Version #2

In the next example, we'll mix a few banters that have been discussed earlier.

🗩 **Conversation:**

Setting: A cozy and friendly atmosphere at a friend's house with people chatting, laughing, and enjoying each other's company.

Isabella: "Nice to meet you, Michael."

Michael: "Of course, you are. As I always say, if you meet me, you have an awesome day!" (Smirks playfully)

Isabella: (laughs) "Well, I'm glad to have an awesome day then!"

Michael: "So, Isabella, tell me, how do you know our friend?"

Isabella: "We met at work. We've been colleagues for a while now."

Michael: "That's great! Work friendships are the best. (pauses) I hope you won't take it personally if I'm not flirting with you right away. First, I must present you to my parents." (winks)

Isabella: (challenging him back) "Oh, really? Parent's approval is required for flirting, huh? I'll be sure to bring my resume and references."

Michael: (laughing) "Deal! They only approve the best. By the way, what's the best thing a guy can say to start flirting with a girl he just met?"

Isabella: (challenging him) "Hmm, that's an interesting question. I'd say something that shows genuine interest in getting to know her."

Michael: (intrigued) "I like that. It should be more about making a connection than trying to impress."

Isabella: "Exactly!"

Michael: (smiling) "Well, in that case, I'm curious, what's your favorite type of cuisine?"

Isabella: "Hmm, I'm quite adventurous. I love trying new things and experimenting with flavors."

Michael: (intrigued) "That's fantastic! Tomorrow, when we go on our second date, I'll take you to a fusion restaurant. And not to impress you. They mix various cuisines to create unique dishes."

Isabella: (playfully) "Oh, are we planning our second date already?"

Michael: (smirks) "Well, why wait? I can't resist good company and eccentric food."

Note: In this example, Michael and Isabella are introduced to each other at a friend's house and engage in playful and friendly banters. He then smoothly transitions into discussing their future plans, playfully suggesting a second date to a fusion restaurant. The interaction showcases their lighthearted chemistry and sets the stage for a potentially enjoyable and exciting connection.

Advice:

Indeed, a few of these playful comments might resemble classic pickup lines, but rest assured, your intention isn't to unleash a grand pickup strategy. Instead, you're weaving humor into the tapestry of conversation, subtly signaling your romantic interest without putting on a grand show. It's like adding a pinch of spice to a dish – just enough to make things interesting, not to blow anyone's taste buds away.

Should the stars align and the girl responds with a dash of sarcasm, don't let it ruffle your feathers. You can counter with a wink and say something like, "Apologies, but I can't resist the allure of pickup lines – they're my secret guilty pleasure" or "You caught me, I do dabble in pickup lines occasionally, but mostly for the sake of my own amusement." With responses like these, you'll navigate the playful banter waters with finesse and charm intact

However, humor is subjective, and some women might not resonate with your playful approach, or they may not be interested in flirting back. If you sense a lack of interest in their reaction, it's essential not to push it. Gracefully change the tone and move the interaction forward without any awkwardness or pressure.

😊 Teasing Remarks

Playful teasing can create a fun and lighthearted atmosphere. Tease her about something light and non-offensive, like her choice of movies or taste in music.

- "You may have interesting taste in music, but I suppose we can still be friends."
- "Your taste in movies is questionable, but I guess we can still

get along."

- "Your fashion sense is unique, but I won't judge... much."
- "Your favorite sports team? Let's agree to disagree, shall we?"
- "I can't believe you like that TV show, but hey, it takes all kinds."
- "Your obsession with pineapple on pizza is a bit alarming, but I'll let it slide."
- "Your sense of humor is something else, but I guess it's growing on me."
- "Your dance moves are... let's call them 'unconventional,' but it's all in good fun."
- "I have to admit, your taste in jokes is questionable, but you make me laugh."
- "You have a unique way of expressing yourself, but that's what makes you interesting."
- "Your choice of books is puzzling, but I suppose it keeps life entertaining."

Note: Teasing lines should be used with care and only in a light-hearted and playful manner, making sure not to offend or hurt anyone's feelings. It's all about having fun and sharing a laugh together.

Flirty Remarks Suitable if She Asks You for Favors

Occasionally, women might ask you to do small favors for them, such as taking their picture or offering a helping hand. Embrace these moments as perfect opportunities to insert some flirty banter by playfully suggesting that they owe you a favor in return. Here are some examples:

- "Well, it's not that simple. First, you must take me out to a romantic dinner and buy my things."

- "Usually, I do this for French kisses, but I'll make an exception for you. You can kiss me on the cheek."
- "Well, I guess I can do that, but only if you promise to be my official hype person for the day."
- "Sure, I'll help you out, but be prepared to owe me a dance at the next party."
- "Alright, I'll do it, but you have to promise to give me a high-five every time we meet from now on."
- "You got it! But in return, you have to share an embarrassing secret."
- "I'll help you with that, but you'll need to give me a grand tour of your favorite spots in the city afterward."
- "Consider it done, but only if you promise to tell me a funny joke that I haven't heard before."
- "Sure thing, but you'll have to teach me one of your impressive skills in return."
- "Okay, I'll help you out, but you'll owe me a round of mini-golf when we hang out next."
- "I'll do it, but you'll have to indulge me in a game of truth or dare later."
- "Sure, but only if you promise to let me win at a friendly game of rock-paper-scissors."
- "Sure, I can do that, but only if you promise to tell a really bad joke afterward."
- "Alright, but be warned, I might need a dance performance in return."
- "I'll be your photographer, but you have to promise to strike your best 'supermodel' pose."
- "Consider it done, but only if you promise not to make it your next profile picture."
- "You got it! But be prepared for a goofy face contest afterward."
- "I'll take the picture, but only if you give me your best 'I'm a

movie star' impression."

- "Okay, I'll help you out, but you better be ready for a photo bomb!"
- "Sure, but I'll need a secret handshake in exchange for my photography skills."

😌 Flirty Lines Suitable for Answering Questions Related to Your Job

At some point, inevitably, she will ask you what you do for a living. To keep the conversation light and playful, you can respond with a flirty remark initially. Here are some examples:

- "I'm not a magician, but I can make a smile appear on your face"
- "I'm not a magician, but I can make your frowns disappear."
- "I'm not a weatherman, but I can promise sunny days when we're together."
- "I'm not a fortune teller, but I see a fun and adventurous future with you."
- "I'm not a chef, but I can cook up some serious chemistry between us."
- "I'm not a mathematician, but I can't count the ways I'm drawn to you."
- "I'm not a detective, but I can't help but investigate your captivating smile."
- "I'm not an artist, but I can draw out some laughter from you."
- "I'm not a pilot, but I'd love to take you on a journey you'll never forget."
- "I'm not a firefighter, but I can ignite a spark between us."
- "I'm not a comedian, but I'm hoping to get a laugh and your number."
- "I'm not an electrician, but I can light up your day."

- "I work in marketing, but my real expertise is selling myself to charming women like you."
- "I'm a chef, but my specialty is cooking up some romance."
- "I'm a software engineer, but my coding skills don't compare to the way you've captivated me."
- "I'm in finance, but my real asset is making you smile."
- "I work in sales, but right now, my only pitch is to win your heart."
- "I'm a teacher, but the subject I excel in is the art of wooing."
- "I'm a photographer, but nothing I've captured compares to your smile."
- "I'm a scientist, but my real experiment is discovering how to make you laugh."

Note: You can also employ such lines if she poses an open-ended question like, "Tell me something about yourself," just before you offer her your genuine response.

😊 Complimentary Flirting

Compliments can be a powerful tool when used effectively. Instead of generic praise, be specific and genuine. For example, compliment her sense of humor, intelligence, or style. Make sure your compliments come across as sincere and not overly flattering.

Compliments can seamlessly integrate into various phases of an interaction, but a savvy approach involves employing them as responses to those occasional yet familiar "Why" inquiries that women often pose when asked for their opinions or assistance. Questions like, "Why do you ask me?" or "Why do you need my opinion?" or "Why do you want me to help you?" can be gracefully met with well-placed compliments.

When giving compliments, it's important not to come across as if you're expecting something in return. This is a common mistake that many guys make. Instead, continue the conversation with playful banter or a teasing remark.

Examples of Remarks that Compliment Her Sense of Humor:

- "I must admit, you have a talent for making me smile. It's like your superpower or something?"
- "I love meeting someone with a good sense of humor. It's like discovering a treasure in a sea of seriousness."
- "I'm convinced you secretly moonlight as a comedian. Your timing is too perfect."
- "They say laughter is contagious, and I think I've caught it from you. You're a walking comedy show!"
- "You must have a degree in humorology because your jokes are seriously top-notch."
- "You have an amazing sense of humor; meeting someone who can make me laugh is refreshing."
- "Your sense of humor is delightful; do you always make people smile?"
- "You're really funny and quick-witted. Your humor adds so much charm to the conversation."
- "Your sense of humor is infectious; I can't help but smile when I'm around you."
- "I must say, your jokes are on point. Your sense of humor is right up my alley."

Note: Complimenting her sense of humor in a genuine and positive way during a first interaction shows that you enjoy her company and find her jokes amusing. Remember to show appreciation for her jokes and funny remarks, as humor is a great way to connect and build rapport. Enjoy the banter and let the conversation naturally unfold from there.

Examples of Remarks that Compliment Her Intelligence:

- "You come across as incredibly intelligent. Your insights during our conversation are impressive."
- "I must say, your knowledge about [topic of discussion] is quite remarkable."
- "Your intelligence is evident; you have a great grasp of various subjects."
- "I'm genuinely fascinated by your intellect and the way you articulate your thoughts."
- "You have such a sharp mind; it's a pleasure to engage in conversation with you."
- "I'm finding your intelligence to be quite captivating. You bring a lot of depth to our discussion."
- "Your curiosity and thoughtful questions really showcase your intelligence."
- "You have a natural ability to grasp complex ideas, and it's quite impressive."
- "Your intelligence shines through in the way you approach things with a rational perspective."
- "I'm enjoying our conversation; your intelligence makes it even more engaging and enriching."

Note: Complimenting her intelligence in a genuine and respectful manner during a first interaction can be a great way to express your admiration for her intellect. Remember to be attentive and actively engage in the conversation to show that you value her insights and ideas. Mutual respect and genuine interest go a long way in creating a meaningful connection.

Examples of Remarks that Compliment Her Style:

- "I must say, you have a great sense of style. Your outfit looks fantastic."

- "You're rocking that look! Your fashion choices are on point."
- "I couldn't help but notice your unique sense of style. It's very impressive."
- "You have a great eye for fashion. Your outfit is so well put together."
- "I love how confident you look in what you're wearing. Your style is really captivating."
- "You have such a cool and laid-back vibe with your style. It suits you perfectly."
- "Your fashion sense is refreshing and stands out in a good way."
- "You look effortlessly stylish. It's clear you know how to dress well."
- "I like how you've added your own personal flair to your outfit. It's very appealing."
- "Your fashion choices reflect a great sense of individuality. I find that really attractive."

Note: Complimenting her style in a simple, genuine, and positive manner can leave a lasting impression. It shows that you notice and appreciate her fashion choices without overwhelming her with excessive flattery.

😊 Compliments with a Twist

Compliments with a twist are unique, clever, and playful compliments that add humor or creativity to traditional praise. They can be effective on women because they stand out from ordinary compliments, capturing their attention and sparking a positive emotional response.

- "Your sense of adventure is unparalleled. I'm ready for any escapade as long as you're my accomplice."

- "Your mind must be an endless playground of creativity. Do you also have a secret lab where you invent futuristic gadgets?"

- "Your smile could give the Mona Lisa a run for her money. It's like a work of art that brightens my day, and I have to wear sunglasses just to look at you!"

- "You're a rare gem in a sea of conformity. It's like finding a hidden treasure in the most unexpected places. Did a pirate hide you here, or did you escape from an ancient treasure chest?"

- "Your taste in music is simply extraordinary. I'm convinced you have a direct line to the DJ of the universe!"

- "Your laughter is contagious. It's like an instant mood-lifter, sure you're not a laughter hypnotist?"

- "You have an incredible sense of style that's uniquely yours. I must admit; I feel like I need to step up my fashion game around you!"

- "Your ability to find humor in any situation is truly impressive. I bet you've been secretly moonlighting as a stand-up comedian!"

- "Your kindness is like a ripple effect. Have you considered launching a 'Random Acts of Kindness' chain reaction?"

- "You have this genuine way of making people feel valued and appreciated. Do you have a special training regimen to keep those positive vibes going?"

Note: Compliments with a twist showcase your wit and charm, making you memorable and leaving a lasting impression on the women you interact with.

😊 Validation Through Comparison Compliments

Such compliments are designed to make a woman stand out from the crowd by highlighting her choices in contrast to those who follow more conventional or shallow paths. They work best when you have learned about her occupation, hobbies, and interests. Validation through comparison is a powerful form of compliment, but it comes with a caveat: it must be sincere. Avoid giving such compliments solely for the sake of doing so.

- "You have a remarkable sense of style that sets you apart from others. Your fashion choices reflect your unique personality and creativity."
- "Wow, while others may chase the spotlight, you're pursuing a career in medicine. Your dedication to helping others truly impresses me."
- "While many follow conventional career paths, your choice to pursue [her profession/passion] shows your determination to carve your own path and make a difference."
- "It's refreshing to meet someone like you who has a passion for science rather than just following the crowd. Your commitment to learning is inspiring."
- "You know, many people dream of fame and fortune, but your love for teaching and education sets you apart. Your desire to make a difference in students' lives is commendable."
- "In a world where everyone seems obsessed with social media, your focus on environmental conservation stands out. Your concern for our planet is praiseworthy."
- "In a world where people often seek validation through social media, you prioritize meaningful experiences and personal growth. Your outlook is truly inspiring."
- "Amidst the pursuit of material success, your passion for charity work is truly remarkable. Your compassion for others is something to be admired."
- "Your dedication to volunteer work and giving back to the community stands out. Your selflessness and empathy make you truly exceptional."

Note: Always remember that the key to effective compliments is to be genuine and specific in your observations. By highlighting her unique qualities and choices, you are acknowledging her individuality and making her feel special.

After offering a validation through comparison compliment, consider following up with some light banter or a teasing remark to keep the interaction playful and engaging. Here is an example:

"You have a remarkable sense of style that sets you apart from others. Your fashion choices reflect your unique personality and creativity. (Pause) However, your taste in movies is questionable, but I guess we can still get along."

😊 Remarks Implying That She's the One Trying to Seduce You

These clever and charming comments add a delightful twist to traditional flattery, making your interactions memorable and enjoyable.

- "You're being quite forward tonight, aren't you? Trying to sweep me off my feet?"
- "I must admit, your attempts at seduction are quite charming, but you'll have to try harder."
- "Oh, you're getting dangerously close to stealing my heart. Nice try!"
- "Is it just me, or are you putting on your best seductive moves tonight?"
- "Well, well, someone's on a mission to make me fall for them. It might just work."
- "I see you've got a bag of tricks to win me over. I'll give you points for effort."
- "Oh, you're quite the smooth talker, but I'm not that easy to charm."

- "You're playing a dangerous game with that irresistible smile. I might have to surrender soon."
- "Trying to make me weak in the knees with your flirty tactics? I'm not falling for it...yet."
- "I must say, your attempts at seducing me are quite entertaining. But I'll resist...for now."
- "Now, you're quite the charmer, but I'll have to resist your seductive ways!"

Note: Such comments should be used in a playful and light-hearted manner to maintain a positive and fun interaction. Use these remarks with a good sense of humor to keep the atmosphere enjoyable for both of you.

Bear in mind that these styles of flirting discussed in this section are meant to cater to a diverse audience, ensuring there's something for everyone's taste. Embrace the freedom to use these flirts sparingly, allowing the conversation to flow naturally without feeling pressured to employ them all at once. Avoid the temptation to memorize these lines verbatim; instead, let them inspire your own unique style of flirting that aligns perfectly with your personality and charm.

Flirting is a delightful way to show interest in a woman and create a connection. Remember to be genuine, respectful, and attentive to her reactions. Every individual is unique, so it's essential to gauge her comfort level and adjust your approach accordingly.

Remember that flirting is not only about words but also about body language. Smiles and eye contact can say a lot about your intentions.

With the right balance of charm, wit, and body language, you can master the art of flirting and leave a lasting impression. Happy flirting!

2. Making Small Talk Count

In the realm of human interactions, there exists a seemingly mundane yet profound practice known as "small talk." Like delicate brushstrokes on a blank canvas, these brief and casual conversations hold the power to pave the way for building emotional connections and unlocking the potential for meaningful relationships, particularly when it comes to connecting with women we've just met.

The significance of small talk lies in its remarkable ability to create an oasis of comfort and familiarity in the vast desert of unfamiliarity. When first encountering someone new, delving straight into profound or personal topics may prove too daunting, causing both parties to retreat behind self-imposed barriers. However, in the gentle realm of small talk, we traverse lightly, testing the waters, and extending a friendly hand of introduction. It's a dance of words, inviting laughter and shared moments, gently unraveling the threads of tension and shyness.

Indeed, when engaging in small talk with women, it is vital to be mindful of the unspoken boundaries and societal nuances. By treading lightly, we demonstrate our respect and sensitivity to their emotional landscape, making them feel at ease to open up gradually. This delicate balance fosters an environment of mutual understanding and trust, allowing the seeds of potential romance to sprout and flourish.

Within the seemingly simple exchanges lie hidden treasures – a glimpse into shared passions and interests that act as bridges between hearts. Through the exchange of thoughts on hobbies, dreams, or even the whimsy of everyday life, we unearth those rare and enchanting moments when two souls recognize the same symphony in their hearts. In these small discussions lies the potential to craft something extraordinary – a relationship built on trust, empathy, and genuine affection. So, let's see some tips on what are the best practices for interesting and flowing small talk.

? How to make small talk

Before we move forward, let's clear up one thing: when I mention small talk, I'm referring to the conversations that follow the delightful banter we explored in the previous section. Prior to diving into small talk, it's advisable to establish a playful foundation. As I've often pointed out, playful conversations set the stage for small talk, small talk leads to meaningful connections, connections pave the way for more intimate gestures, intimacy introduces the prospect of a relationship, and a relationship... well, you get the idea! But hey, someone please pull the brakes before I keep going! So, after a few minutes of playful conversation, it's time to delve into getting to know each other better. Here's how:

❶ How to Start

While there isn't a precise formula for initiating small talk, based on my experience, it's often advantageous to commence the conversation by discussing hobbies and passions. Subsequently, topics related to occupations and other subjects can naturally follow. Nevertheless, there might be instances where a woman asks about your profession right away. In such cases, your respective jobs become the primary topic of discussion. Indeed, when the conversation revolves around work, it's generally advisable to let her initiate the query about your occupation, rather than the other way around.

❷ How to Craft Questions About Her Job and Interests

When seeking to uncover her interests or profession, it's advisable to steer clear of mundane inquiries such as "What do you do for a living?" or "Do you have any passions?" Instead, aim to employ intriguing or light-hearted approaches. Here are a few illustrative examples:

To learn her passions and hobbies:

- "What kind of activities do you enjoy during your free time?"
- "When you have free time, how do you like to spend it?"
- "So, tell me, do you have any hidden talents or hobbies I should know about?"
- "So, tell me something interesting about yourself. What's your hidden talent or a quirky hobby?"
- "Tell me about a hobby or activity that truly captivates your interest."
- "Aside from being such a cutie, what else do you do in your free time?"
- "Do you have any passions that might surprise someone at first glance?"
- "When you're looking to unwind and recharge, what kind of activities do you turn to?"

If you want to maintain the conversation in the hobbies aria you can ask her if she has any future goals:

- "As you think about the future, are there any hobbies or interests you'd like to explore or deepen?"

If the first topic was about work, you can continue with...

- "So, aside from your work, are there any other things that truly light up your day?"
- "So, when you're not busy with work, what activities do you enjoy pursuing?"
- "How do you unwind after work?"
- "When you're not working, how do you make the most of

your weekdays and find fulfillment?"

- "Apart from work, what else do you find satisfying?"
- "Your dedication to your work is impressive. But I'm curious, beyond work, what activities do you find most fulfilling?"
- "It's clear that you're quite accomplished in your career. Beyond that, what are the things that bring you joy in your life?"

To learn her job:

- "So, what about you... What keeps you busy and fulfilled during your weekdays?"
- "Tell me, what's your weekday playground where you make things happen?"
- "What about you, in which domain do you weave your magic?"
- "What occupies your time and expertise when the sun is up?"
- "When you're not chasing dreams, what's your professional playground?"
- "What's your main focus when the day begins and tasks unfold?"
- "What do you dive into during working hours, if you don't mind sharing?"
- "What's the area you specialize in when the clock starts ticking?"
- "Where does your expertise come to life as the day unfolds?"
- "When responsibilities call, what's the field where you shine?"
- "What's your go-to domain when the sun rises and work begins?"

Note: Employing these types of questions can render the interaction more captivating, steering clear of sounding like an interrogation.

❸ How to Craft Responses About Your Work or Interests

☞ Offer Elaborated Responses

In face-to-face interactions, it's advisable to enrich your answers. For example, if she inquiries about your hobbies and, let's say, you enjoy reading, refrain from a simple reply like, "I like to read." Opt for something more engaging such as: "Well, I have a bit of a nerdy side. In my free time, I love to lose myself in the pages of a good fantasy novel. There's just something magical about those worlds that captivate me." If your profession, let's say, involves graphic design, consider sharing something like: "I work as a graphic designer; it's a realm of ceaseless creativity and deadlines. Yet, as the saying goes, one should do what they love, don't you think?" Steering clear of simply saying, "I'm just a [job title]" is advisable. Strive to expand your responses and discuss your vocation and passions with fervor.

☞ Anticipate open-ended inquiries

Instead of kicking off with run-of-the-mill job-related queries, she might throw something more open like "Tell me something about yourself." A stellar reply to such questions would be a blend of your history, present, and future, e.g., "Well, I've got a mix of stories in my life's scrapbook. Back in the day, I was all about skateboarding and trying to master those tricks. These days, I'm diving into marketing campaigns, trying to make a splash in the digital world. Looking ahead, I'm dreaming of backpacking across Europe, soaking in the culture and savoring every moment. How about you? What's your tale?"

⚷ Avoid Negativity

The path of negativity is one to be bypassed. Avoid voicing griev-
ances about your job, superiors, colleagues, or clients. Even if your
job isn't your favorite, you could, for instance, highlight how your
work positively impacts others: "While sales may not be my dream
job, I take pride in the positive impact it has on others. Finding so-
lutions that genuinely benefit my clients and seeing how it improves
their lives or businesses is a rewarding aspect of what I do. It makes
the job worthwhile."

❹ How to Navigate Topic Duration

Successful conversations with women during initial interactions
aren't about engaging in debates on specific subjects; they're about
establishing an introductory understanding of each other. During
this phase, delving excessively into particular work-related or
hobby-related aspects isn't necessary. For instance, if she shares her
fondness for romantic comedy movies, you needn't extensively discuss romantic comedies. Instead, a transition might sound like this:
"Some of those can be quite entertaining, but I'm more of a science
fiction enthusiast. Speaking of preferences, do you have a go-to
song when you start your day?" However, if the hobby is intriguing,
such as travel or volunteering, delving a bit deeper is permissible.

Similarly, work-related topics shouldn't monopolize the conversation. If she mentions her occupation, avoid probing into specific
work details. For instance, if she's a nurse, abstain from inquiring
about the number of injections she administers daily. Opt for a line
of conversation like: "Was this your aspiration all along or did it
unfold unexpectedly?" or "What was your dream job when you were
a little girl?" Naturally, you can explore the aspects that attract both
you and her to the respective occupation or interest, but evading
excessive minutiae is advised. Keep in mind, the focus is on mutual
discovery and understanding.

❺ How to Avoid that Awkward Silence

☞ Focus only on her

The cardinal principle in conversing with any woman is to "engage with presence," that is, to direct your undivided attention to her. When she addresses you, listen closely, setting aside thoughts of your own forthcoming words. Every syllable she articulates serves as a clue, from which you can weave intricate connections. However, if your mind wanders elsewhere or you preoccupy yourself with planning your next response during her discourse, you'll overlook those cues, risking a conversational impasse.

☞ Give Engaging Responses

Whenever a woman shares something with you, ensure your response is composed of either an assertion, an insight, a query, a narrative, or even a joke.

Examples:

- "So, your opinion is [insert her opinion]. Interesting. Why do you think this?"
- "Oh, that's really interesting. What else can you tell me?"
- "That's fascinating! Tell me more, please."
- "This reminds me of an incident that occurred a few years ago... [share the incident]"
- "Something similar happened 'to me' or 'to a friend of mine'... [narrate what happened]"
- "This is just like in that joke... [tell the joke]"

⊶ Ask Open-Ended Questions

Ensure that the questions you pose are open-ended. This implies that they should elicit responses of at least a single sentence. Therefore, unless you have a follow-up question or statement, avoid asking questions that could be answered with simple responses like "yes," "no," "maybe," "fine," or other brief words.

Examples:

- "What do you enjoy doing when you're not at work?"
- "Tell me about any interesting hobbies you've discovered lately."
- "What's your go-to spot for grabbing a bite to eat around here?"
- "Can you recommend a great book or movie you've enjoyed recently?"
- "How do you usually like to spend your weekends?"
- "Have you been on any exciting trips or vacations recently? Where did you go?"
- "Could you share a memorable event or party you've attended?"
- "Are there any upcoming plans or events you're looking forward to?"
- "What's your favorite way to unwind after a busy day?"
- "Have you come across any interesting local events or festivals?"

These questions encourage open-ended responses, allowing the conversation to flow more naturally during small talk interactions.

⚷ Provide Expansive Responses to Closed Questions

When she poses questions that could be swiftly answered with just a single word, seize the opportunity to offer a more comprehensive and detailed reply.

💬 Examples:

Closed Question: "Did you have a good weekend?"
Expansive Answer: "Yes, I had a wonderful weekend! On Saturday, I went hiking with friends in a nearby nature reserve, and then on Sunday, I tried out a new recipe I found online and spent some quality time reading."

Closed Question: "Did you catch that new movie everyone's talking about?"
Expansive Answer: "No, I haven't had a chance to see it yet. Lately, I've been engrossed in a novel that a friend recommended, and it's been a captivating read."

Closed Question: "Do you enjoy traveling?"
Expansive Answer: "Absolutely, traveling is one of my favorite things to do. Exploring new places, immersing myself in different cultures, and trying local cuisine really energize me. One of the most memorable trips I've had was backpacking through Europe last summer."

Closed Question: "Do you enjoy going to big social gatherings?"
Expansive Answer: "No, I'm not really into big social gatherings. I find that I connect better in smaller settings, like cozy get-

togethers with friends, where I can have meaningful conversations."

Closed Question: "Are you into sports?"
Expansive Answer: "Definitely, I'm quite passionate about sports. I regularly play tennis and also enjoy attending basketball games. Last summer, I even participated in a local charity run, which was a fantastic experience."

Closed Question: "Do you have a favorite genre of music?"
Expansive Answer: "Not really, my music taste is quite eclectic. I enjoy everything from classical compositions to modern indie tracks. Depending on my mood, I might be listening to jazz or a catchy pop song."

Note: These detailed answers provide insights into the person's preferences and experiences while expanding on their response to closed questions, creating a richer and more engaging conversation. Any part of your response can become the basis for the next topic of conversation.

☞ Reciprocate with Her Questions

When she poses a question that she hasn't answered herself previously, always reciprocate by asking the same question in return. When you reciprocate with the same question, ensure that you rephrase it in an open-ended format.

💬 Examples:

Question: "Are you a fan of outdoor adventures?"
Answer: "No, I'm not really an outdoorsy person. However, I appreciate the beauty of nature and occasionally enjoy leisurely walks in scenic parks to unwind."

Reciprocate: "What about you? When and where did you have your last outdoor adventures?"

Question: "Do you like reading?"
Answer: "Yes, reading is a big part of my life. I'm drawn to both fiction and non-fiction and lately, I've been diving into historical novels and psychology books. The insights I gain from reading often influence my perspective on various aspects of life."
Reciprocate: "What about you? What was the last book you delved into?"

Question: "Do you like attending live music concerts?"
Answer: "No, I'm not really a big concertgoer. However, I do occasionally attend smaller acoustic performances at local venues, as they offer a more intimate experience."
Reciprocate: "What about you? What live concerts did you attend lately?"

⌗ Echo Her Last Word as a Question

If you find yourself momentarily at a loss for words when it's your turn to respond, an effective approach is to rephrase the last one or two words of her previous statement into an interrogative form. This subtle technique encourages her to share more details, providing you with cues to maintain a smooth and engaging conversation flow. Let's take a closer look at how this tactic unfolds:

Girl: "I have a fascination for ancient history."
Guy: "Ancient history?"
Girl: "Definitely, delving into the past helps me understand the world we live in today."
Guy: "It's fascinating how our present is shaped by what came before. Do you have a particular era that captivates you the most?"

Girl: "Absolutely, I'm really drawn to the Renaissance period. The explosion of art, culture, and ideas during that time is incredibly inspiring."

Guy: "The Renaissance was indeed a remarkable period. I've always been intrigued by the influence of historical events on art and creativity. What other forms of art do you appreciate?"

Note: In this example, the guy seamlessly transitions from the repeated question into deeper aspects of the girl's interests, exploring her preferences and experiences related to history and art.

Typically, two or three repetitions suffice to uncover cues that facilitate the flow of interaction. Thus, it's advisable not to overutilize this technique.

Example:

Girl: "I've been practicing meditation to reduce stress."
Guy: "Stress?"
Girl: "Indeed, meditation has been a transformative practice that brings calmness to my busy life."
Guy: "Busy life?"
Girl: "Absolutely, between work, personal projects, and spending time with family, it sometimes feels like there's never a dull moment."
Guy: "I can imagine. How did you discover meditation as a way to cope?"
Girl: "Well, a friend recommended it during a particularly hectic time, and it surprised me how much it resonated. It's like a reset button for my mind. How about you? How do you unwind when things get busy?"
Guy: "I find solace in reading and going for long walks. It helps clear my mind and provides a sense of balance."

Note: In this example, the conversation naturally flows from the guy's repeated question, leading to deeper insights about the girl's experiences and eventually transitioning to a question about the guy's own methods of relaxation.

☞ Share Humor

In the event that those occasional lulls in conversation arise, there's no need to fret. It's entirely natural for such moments to occur during interactions. For instances like these, it's valuable to have a couple of brief jokes prepared to share. I've discovered that employing setup-punchline jokes that play on gender-related stereotypes and the common dynamics between men and women can be particularly fitting for engaging with women.

Example:

Guy: "Do you know how a woman apologizes to a man?"
Girl: "Well, I can't recall doing such a thing, so I don't know."
Guy: "I'm sorry, but it was your fault."
Girl: "Hahaha, right!"
Guy: "Now it's your turn…"
Girl: "For what?"
Guy: "To tell me a good joke."
Girl: "I can't think of any jokes right now."
Guy: "Then I'll tell you one more while you think about it."

Let's explore a few similar jokes that can be seamlessly integrated into conversations:

- ☺ "Ever notice how men apologize to women? 'I'm sorry, but you made me do it."
- ☺ "You know how women give advice to men? 'You should have done it this way."

☺ "Have you heard how men react when women ask for directions? 'Sure, let's take the scenic route."

☺ "Ever noticed how women respond to men's cooking? 'It's good, but I would have added some spices."

☺ "You know how men listen to women's stories? 'I was halfway through before I remembered to nod."

Note: As with all jokes, it's important to use them in appropriate and light-hearted settings.

☞ Transit to playful conversations

Employ teasing remarks, compliments with a playful twist, or any flirtatious approach that fits the context to shift the conversation back to a lighthearted tone. Not only does this skill aid in addressing awkward silences, but it also infuses a shift in the interaction dynamic, enhancing its overall enjoyment. Therefore, alternating between small talk topics and playful conversations is a seamless strategy, even when not solely aimed at resolving moments of potential silence.

🗨 A Small Talk Example:

Setting: After a few minutes of playful conversation.

Riley: "So, Liam, what do you do for a living?"
Liam: "Well, I'm not a fortune teller, but I see a fun and adventurous future with you."
Riley: (grinning) "Oh, that's quite the prediction, Liam."
Liam: (smirking) "Well, a little mystery adds excitement, right?"
Riley: (laughs) "I can't argue with that. So, tell me, what's your profession?"
Liam: (enthusiastically) "I'm a programmer. I dive into lines of code, building applications, and solving digital puzzles. It might

sound geeky, but I approach it with fervor. Speaking the language of machines can be its own kind of adventure. And speaking of adventures, what keeps you busy and fulfilled during your weekdays, Riley?"

Riley: (animatedly) "I work in marketing. It's all about crafting stories, shaping perceptions, and navigating the dynamic world of consumer behavior."

Liam: (impressed) "That sounds like quite the creative challenge. Did you always know this is what you wanted, or did it unfold unexpectedly?"

Riley: (reflectively) "Funny enough, I thought I'd end up in a completely different field. But life had its own plans, and I'm glad it led me here."

Liam: (nodding) "Life has its twists, indeed. So, when the workday winds down, what passions do you pursue?"

Riley: (enthusiastically) "I'm all about exploring new places, whether it's hopping on a plane or discovering hidden gems in the city. I also love hanging out with friends and practicing yoga to keep that work-life balance."

Liam: (intrigued) "Traveling, friendships, and yoga, a vibrant mix. As for me, I'm a fan of cycling through scenic trails, hiking to breathtaking views, spending quality time with friends, and, believe it or not, I play the drums."

Riley: (playfully surprised) "Oh, a drummer! Now that's an unexpected twist."

Liam: (teasingly) "Well, someone's got to keep the rhythm in life, right?"

Riley: (laughs) "Touché, Liam."

Liam: (smirking) "You know, I think your marketing skills might come in handy to promote my drumming performances."

Riley: (raising an eyebrow) "Hmm, I'll have to see if the world is ready for a programmer-drummer fusion."

Liam: (grinning) "Hey, it's all about innovation, isn't it?"

Riley: (laughs) "True, but let's not cause a genre clash just yet."

Liam: (playfully dramatic) "Alright, I'll save the fusion for later. But if you change your mind, I'll be here, drumming up a storm."
Riley: (teasingly) "I'll keep that in mind, maestro."
Liam: (smiling) "So tell me, are there any upcoming plans or events you're looking forward to?"

Note: In this playful and engaging dialog, Liam and Riley share insights about their professions and passions, transitioning seamlessly from discussing work to personal interests. The dialog showcases their personalities, interests, and a bit of playful teasing, setting the foundation for further interactions.

Remember, the heart of small talk isn't just about being concise, it's like the finely crafted dance moves of a squirrel trying to impress other squirrels at a tree party. Active listening and genuine interest are the secret spices in this delightful conversational stew. It's like showing someone that their words are the juiciest berries you've ever encountered in the forest.

In the enchanted realm of small talk, we're like wizards wielding the wand of attention, conjuring genuine connections out of thin air. It's as if we're saying, "Your thoughts are my spells, and I'm all ears!" And let's face it, in a world buzzing with distractions, giving someone your full attention is practically a magical spell in itself.

Think of small talk as a mischievous gnome leading you on a treasure hunt for shared experiences. With a sprinkle of humor, you turn dull moments into gems of connection. It's like finding a secret door in the conversational labyrinth that opens up to laughter, shared quirks, and inside jokes only the two of you understand.

Within these fleeting exchanges, we're like Sherlock Holmes, picking up on subtle clues of compatibility. The raised eyebrow, the twinkling gaze – they're like Morse code from the heart. And oh, the allure of her laughter – it's like music composed just for you, inviting you to dance to the rhythm of connection.

So, my fellow adventurer in conversation, let's wield the art of small talk with finesse. These seemingly unassuming interactions are like seeds that sprout into rich discussions. And speaking of rich conversations, let's dive into the skill of forging connections that can withstand the storms of life – it's like crafting armor for our hearts against the chaos of the world.

3. Chats that Matter: The Meaningful Talk

The art of building deep connections with women! It's like mastering a dance that weaves through the intricate steps of understanding, respect, and genuine interest. Picture this: you've engaged in lighthearted banter, explored each other's quirks, and even swapped stories about work, hobbies, and passions. You've waded through the introductory tides and established a solid, surface-level connection. But now, you're standing at the edge of the deep waters – the realm where interactions transform from casual discussions to meaningful connections that resonate on a profound level.

In this section, we're about to embark on a journey that goes beyond the realm of small talk and enters the realm of heartfelt dialogues. Building deep connections with women isn't a scripted formula; it's a skill that requires genuine interest, active participation, and a dash of your unique charm. We'll delve into practical strategies that can transition your conversations from light and playful to profound and resonant.

Remember, at this stage, you're not just engaging in chit-chat; you're crafting the foundation for a bond that can weather life's storms and celebrate its joys. It's time to infuse your conversations with authenticity, vulnerability, and a genuine desire to understand and be understood.

But wait! Why does all this connection-building matter? Because the ripples of deep connections spread wider than the latest viral meme. When you truly connect with a woman, you're not just enriching her life – you're enriching yours. You're fostering trust, companionship, and the kind of camaraderie that can weather life's storms. So, put on your dancing shoes, my friend. The art of building deep connections with women is a masterpiece in the making.

So, my connection-seeking friend, let's unravel the secrets of building deep connections after the initial banter has paved the way. Get ready to master the art of transitioning from playful small talk conversation to discussions that touch the core of who you both are.

Now, let's set sail and explore the practical strategies that will guide you toward the depths of meaningful connection.

? How to Craft Deeper Connections

℅ Embrace the "Receive and Give" Dynamic

While the art of building profound connections with women isn't confined to rigid scripts, it involves a straightforward principle: "Receive and Give." In essence, when she entrusts you with a personal insight, it's your cue to reciprocate with something personal and relevant to the conversation. This sharing could take the form of an opinion, a statement, or an experience akin to the one she shared. It's important to note that this experience needn't be exclusively yours; it might encompass the encounters of those close to you. So, keep in mind that every time she responds to your inquiries, it's an invitation for you to reciprocate, enriching the exchange, and when appropriate, engaging further through follow-up questions.

℅ Recall and Reference: Building Bridges with Shared Memories

Imagine you're chatting with her and something she mentioned during the small talk phase tugs at your memory. Maybe it's her enthusiasm for hiking, or for baking escapades; it doesn't matter. Bring it up and watch the magic unfold.

Examples:

- "I remember you talking about your passion for baking. Have you whipped up any delectable creations recently? I'd love to hear more about your culinary adventures."
- "I remember you mentioned your love for travel. Tell me about a travel experience that exceeded your expectations completely."
- "I remember you mentioning your fascination with history. Exploring the stories that have shaped our world can be so enlightening. Are there any specific historical periods or events that you find particularly captivating?"

☛ Shared Experiences: Weaving Bonds Through Common Interests

You both found a shared passion for a particular interest. Build upon that by asking about her most memorable experience related to that interest.

Examples:

- "Our shared interest in volunteering got me thinking – can you share a volunteer experience that left a lasting impact on you?"
- "Our shared interest in outdoor activities sparked my curiosity. Have you ever had an adventure that pushed you out of your comfort zone? It could be a hiking trip, a daring rock-climbing experience, or anything that made your heart race."

- ● "Our mutual appreciation for music got me thinking – do you have a go-to song that never fails to uplift your mood?"
- ● "Our passion for travel caught my attention. Is there a destination that surprised you with its unique culture and traditions?"

After she responds, share your experience too, or if you prefer, you can take the lead by sharing your story first and then encourage her to share a similar experience. Let's see an illustration of that:

- ● "Regarding our passion for travel, I had this incredible travel experience that completely exceeded my expectations. I went on a hiking trip to the Grand Canyon, and what made it truly unforgettable was a chance encounter with a group of local wildlife experts. They invited me to join them on a sunrise hike, and as we reached a breathtaking vista, they began to share their deep knowledge about the ecosystem. Watching the sun paint the canyon walls with vivid colors while listening to their stories about the area's unique flora and fauna was a surreal moment. What about you? What's a travel experience that left you in awe?"

☞ Story Time: Opening Up Through Personal Anecdotes

Your conversations are like storybooks, each page revealing more about your lives. Share a personal experience that connects to what she's discussed. Let's say she discussed her fascination with underwater exploration. You could share, "Your fascination with underwater exploration reminded me of a snorkeling adventure I had in the Great Barrier Reef. The colors and marine life were absolutely breathtaking."

☞ Dreams and Aspirations: Peering into Tomorrow's Horizons

You've exchanged tales of today; now it's time to gaze into the future. What are her dreams? What adventures does she yearn for?

Examples:

- 🎤 "You've mentioned a bit about your journey so far. Looking ahead, are there any dreams or goals you're still eager to pursue? It could be something you've been thinking about for a while or a newfound interest, I'd love to hear about it."

If she mentioned her aspiration to travel the world, you could ask:

- 🎤 "I remember you mentioning your wanderlust. Imagine you have a magical plane ticket that can take you anywhere in the world. The catch? It's a one-way ticket to your dream destination. Where would you go and what experiences do you envision awaiting you there?"

☞ Opinions and Insights: Navigating Meaningful Conversations

Shift towards more meaningful topics. Discuss recent news, trends, or thought-provoking questions. Asking her opinion on something important engages her intellectually and reveals her deeper thoughts. However, it's best to avoid delving too deeply into intellectual topics. Remember, this is a "get-to-know-each-other" interaction, not a trivia contest.

Examples:

○ Ask about her take on recent news or a subject you both have discussed. "I read an article about sustainable fashion, and it made me think of our conversation on ethical choices. What are your thoughts on how individuals can make a positive impact through their fashion choices?"

○ During a discussion about global perspectives, you share your admiration for cultures that emphasize community harmony. You might ask, "Considering the diverse cultures we've talked about, which cultural value or tradition resonates with you the most, and why?"

○ As you talk about relationships, you express your belief in open communication as a key foundation. You might inquire, "What's your take on the role of communication in maintaining healthy relationships? Are there cultural differences you've noticed in how people approach this?"

○ As you discuss social issues, you mention your admiration for individuals who actively advocate for positive change. You could ask, "In today's world, what's a cause that you feel passionately about and believe deserves more attention?"

○ During a conversation about sustainability, you talk about your appreciation for cultures that have a strong connection to nature. You could ask, "Do you think there's a cultural approach to environmental conservation that the rest of the world could learn from?"

☛ Ask Open-Ended Questions: The Gateway to Deeper Dialogues

Just as in small talk discussions, in meaningful conversations, we also apply the same principle of shifting from yes-or-no questions to those that invite her to share more. Open-ended questions encourage thoughtful responses.

Examples:

- "What inspired you to start [interest]?"
- "What do you find most rewarding about [interest]?"
- "How did you choose your current job?"
- "How would your dream destination look like?"
- "What story from your past always brings a smile to your face?"
- "Tell me about a recent accomplishment that made you proud."
- "What's something on your mind that you're eager to explore further?"
- "What's a place you've been to that left you with lasting memories?"
- "What's an experience you've had recently that gave you a new perspective or made you think about something in a different way?"

If she's confused by a question, you can help her a little bit, e.g., "It could be anything... a small detail or an interesting encounter, I'm curious to hear about the moments that shape our outlook."

⊶ Emotionally Relatable Topics: Sharing Vulnerabilities

Now, picture this: You're sharing a personal story, a tale of triumph, or even a moment of vulnerability. It's like showing her your superhero cape – flawed, yet wonderfully real. Vulnerability isn't weakness; it's your secret weapon. It creates a safe space for her to open up, building a bond that's stronger than Superman's grip.

Gently touch on emotions, like challenges she's faced or moments of triumph. Sharing vulnerabilities fosters intimacy and opens the door to deeper conversations.

Examples:

📖 Suppose she mentions her struggle with learning a new language. You could share, "I once tried to learn French, and the pronunciation had me tongue-tied! What keeps you motivated to keep learning?"

📖 During a conversation about embracing challenges, she opens up about how stepping out of her comfort zone has transformed her life. You could share, "It reminded me of a significant crossroads when I chose to backpack solo through Europe – an experience that reshaped my perspective. Have you ever ventured beyond your comfort zone, perhaps into a new place or experience, and found it to be unexpectedly transformative?"

📖 During a discussion about work-life equilibrium, you share insights into the challenges of harmonizing professional ambitions with personal commitments: "It takes me back to a period when I was working full-time while also pursuing a degree at night school. This demanding schedule taught me valuable time management skills and the importance of setting priorities. Have you ever balanced demanding commitments, and what strategies did you employ to ensure you didn't burn out?"

📖 You could open a dialogue about making life choices within the context of family dynamics, where you share about the intricate balance between personal aspirations and familial bonds: "It reminds me of a significant moment when I decided to pursue a career in art instead of the more traditional path my family envisioned. Have you ever stood at a crossroads where your ambitions diverged from those of your family, and how did you navigate it?"

📖 While discussing the essence of resilience, she mentions how setbacks can lead to unforeseen opportunities. You could share, "This brings to mind a time when I was pursuing a career in law, and an unexpected job loss led me to explore a different field entirely – eventually leading to a fulfilling career in marketing. Have you encountered other setbacks that prompted you to explore a new direction, ultimately leading to a positive outcome?"

⌐ Dig Deeper: Uncovering Motivations

When she talks about a hobby or passion, inquire about the deeper reasons behind it. Understanding the motivations behind her interests can reveal a lot about her values and experiences, fostering a richer connection between the two of you. Unveiling the meaning behind her pursuits can lead to more meaningful conversations and a deeper understanding of her personality.

Examples:

- ♀ If she mentioned her photography hobby, you can inquire about the deeper motivations behind it. "When you're taking photos, do you have a specific emotion you want to capture in each shot? I'm curious about the story behind the lens."
- ♀ If she's into painting, ask what emotions she aims to convey through her art: "Could you share what themes or ideas often inspire your artistic creations? I'm curious to know what drives your creativity."
- ♀ If she talks about her love for hiking and how she often explores different trails, you could say, "It's fascinating to hear about your passion for hiking. When you embark on a new trail, is there a particular aspect of nature that draws you in and motivates your choice?"

⚬ During the conversation, she shares her enthusiasm for volunteering at animal shelters: "Volunteering at animal shelters sounds incredibly rewarding. Is there a specific experience or encounter that initially inspired you to dedicate your time to this cause?"

⚬ She expresses her interest in playing musical instruments, specifically the piano: "Playing musical instruments requires dedication. Is there a particular emotion or mood you enjoy expressing through your piano playing, or perhaps a piece of music that deeply resonates with you?"

⚬ The same goes for her job: "So, you mentioned earlier that you are a physician. Is it something you always wanted to be, or did someone else influence your decision?"

⚬━ Personal Growth: Exploring the Path of Development

Discuss personal growth and development. Ask about a book that's influenced her or inquire about a skill she'd love to develop. These conversations reveal her values and aspirations.

Examples:

✈ During a discussion about hobbies, she mentioned her interest in astronomy. You could ask, "Is there a particular book or resource that inspired your curiosity about the cosmos?"

✈ During a conversation about facing adversity, you share how a difficult experience taught you resilience. You might ask, "In your journey, what's a challenge you've overcome that has significantly shaped your personal growth?"

✈ While discussing personal journeys, you admit to making mistakes that turned into valuable life lessons. You could inquire, "Have you had a moment where a mistake led to a valuable insight that contributed to your personal development?"

🏹 As you delve into hobbies, you share your passion for learning musical instruments. You might ask, "Is there a skill or interest you've always wanted to pursue but haven't yet? What holds you back, and how do you plan to overcome it?"

🏹 During a conversation about wellness, you express your interest in mindfulness practices. You could inquire, "Have you explored mindfulness techniques, and do you find any specific ones particularly effective in promoting personal growth?"

⚷ Listen, Listen, Listen

As you progress, remember the golden rule of active listening. Imagine you're watching the latest blockbuster – your eyes are glued to the screen, right? Apply the same enthusiasm to listening. Nod, smile, let her know you're right there with her. No interrupting, no plotting your response while she talks. It's like giving her the VIP seat in the theater of your attention.

⚷ Cultivate Empathy and Understanding

Picture this: You're chatting with a woman, and suddenly, you're not just hearing her words, you're feeling her emotions. That's the magic of empathy, my friend. When you can truly put yourself in her shoes, you're building bridges of connection stronger than Spider-Man's webs. Understanding her joys, fears, and dreams makes her feel seen and valued.

Engage with her responses, show empathy, and respond thoughtfully. This creates an atmosphere of trust and understanding.

Examples:

☼ As you discuss hobbies, she expresses her passion for painting. You respond with genuine interest, saying, "It's fascinating how painting can capture emotions. Could you tell me about a painting that you feel truly reflects a powerful feeling?"

☼ In a conversation about her profession, she talks about the challenges of her field. You respond empathetically, "I can imagine how demanding that must be. What's one thing that keeps you motivated even during the toughest times?"

☼ During a conversation about personal growth, she opens up about a difficult experience. You respond empathetically, saying, "I can see how that situation would shape your perspective. How did you manage to find strength and positivity during that time?"

☼ As she discusses her cultural background, you express genuine curiosity, saying, "It's really interesting to learn about your traditions. Could you share a moment from your culture that holds a special place in your heart?"

☼ During your conversation, she mentions her upcoming art exhibition and her excitement is evident in her voice. This is a perfect opportunity to show your interest and engage her in a deeper conversation: "I can sense the excitement in your voice when you talk about your upcoming art exhibition. How are you feeling as the big day approaches?"

☙ Quality Over Quantity: Patience in Building Connections

Remember, you are not playing 20 Questions here. Instead of firing off questions like you're in a rapid-fire interview, take a breath and dive deeper. The goal is to show you're genuinely interested, not that you're conducting an FBI interrogation.

Deep connections aren't rushed; they evolve over time. Allow the conversation to unfold naturally, letting topics surface organically. When she shares a story, resist the urge to abruptly switch subjects. Instead, dive deeper into that story with follow-up questions.

🗨 Examples:

Context: She talks about how she enjoys spending weekends exploring new hiking trails in the nearby mountains.
Follow-up Question: "Exploring hiking trails sounds like a great way to unwind. Do you have any favorite trails that you find yourself returning to?"

Context: She mentions her passion for photography and how she enjoys capturing the beauty of everyday moments.
Follow-up Question: "Photography is such a creative outlet. Is there a particular subject or setting that you find most inspiring to photograph?"

Context: The conversation turns to cooking, and she shares how experimenting with different recipes has become a fun hobby for her.
Follow-up Question: "Cooking experiments can lead to some surprising dishes. What's one unique combination you've tried that turned out surprisingly delicious?"

Context: She expresses her love for live music and how attending concerts is a source of joy for her.
Follow-up Question: "Live concerts have a unique energy. Have you ever attended a concert that left you with a memorable experience or story?"

Context: She talks about her interest in reading and how books transport her to different worlds.

Follow-up Question: "Books can be such powerful escapes. Is there a particular book that resonated with you on a deep level or perhaps changed your perspective?"

⚷ Negativity: The No-to-Go Path

Steer clear of discussions centered around frustrations, complaints, disappointments, or any other emotional baggage. While these topics may find a home on a therapist's couch, they're not the foundation for forging deep and meaningful connections.

Feel free to share a story that involves a touch of negativity, but only if it has a triumphant resolution and no longer carries any lingering negativity. For instance, if she mentions that her parents influenced her to pursue a career in medicine, you can connect by sharing a similar experience that has since evolved and no longer impacts you negatively: "I can definitely relate. My father was a colonel, and he had his heart set on me becoming a soldier just like him. I even got through a military academy; eventually, I realized that a military career wasn't my calling. These days, I find myself thriving in a multinational company, and the satisfaction I derive from my work is truly fulfilling."

Examples of questions great for starting or continuing deep connection interactions:

- "Do you get along well with your parents?"
- "What's the most beautiful memory you have with your siblings?"
- "What's the most significant thing your family has given you?"
- "When you were young, were you encouraged to try new things or did you feel restricted?"
- "What role does spirituality play in your life?"

- "What experience has brought you the greatest joy?"
- "What gives you the most hope?"
- "What would you like to achieve in order to feel that you have a fulfilled life?"
- "What's your oldest memory?"
- "Are there any family stories about when you were a baby?"
- "What's the biggest trouble you've gotten into so far?"
- "What's your greatest fear when it comes to the future?"

These questions touch on personal experiences, emotions, and values, which are key aspects of building meaningful connections. They can help foster open and insightful conversations that allow individuals to share more about themselves and their perspectives, ultimately strengthening the bond between them.

Remember, your conversation partner isn't sitting for an interview, so don't overwhelm her with the entire list of questions in a single interaction! Select a few of them, and then explore the answer she shares in more depth. It's also wise to have your own response ready for the same question, just in case she reciprocates the inquiry.

💬 Example of a meaningful conversation starter

Setting: After a playful small talk conversation.

Patrick: "I remember you mentioned your love for travel. Tell me about a travel experience that exceeded your expectations completely."

Siobhan: (Excited) "Oh, absolutely! I went on a solo trip to Japan last year, and it turned out to be a life-changing experience. The culture, the food, the scenery – everything was so different and fascinating."

Patrick: (Engaged) "Japan sounds incredible. I've always been drawn to the idea of experiencing a completely different culture. Actually, a couple of years back, I ventured into Thailand, and I was amazed at how vibrant and diverse everything was."

Siobhan: "Wow, that must have been amazing! So, what was the most unforgettable moment of your trip?"

Patrick: "Well, one evening in Bangkok, I stumbled upon a local food market. The aroma of the street food was irresistible, and I found myself bonding with the locals over our shared love for cuisine. It was a fantastic way to connect with the place."

Siobhan: (Enthusiastic) "That's the best part of traveling – those unexpected connections you make. By the way, my Japan trip was filled with those moments too. I remember meeting a group of locals who taught me origami in a park, and we ended up chatting for hours."

Patrick: (Curious) "Origami sounds like a unique way to connect. Speaking of unexpected connections, do you have a travel destination on your bucket list that you're really excited about exploring?"

Siobhan: (Thoughtful) "Definitely Iceland. I'm captivated by its natural beauty and the aurora borealis. It's a dream to experience that kind of magic."

Patrick: (Enthusiastic) "Iceland is on my list too! It's incredible how nature can be so awe-inspiring. You know, I've always been drawn to the idea of exploring places that have a strong connection to nature, like the Swiss Alps. Have you ever considered visiting them?"

Siobhan: (Engaged) "The Swiss Alps sound amazing, and I love the idea of being surrounded by nature. It's funny how travel opens up these possibilities you never really thought about."

Patrick: (Smiling) "Absolutely, it's like each adventure uncovers new facets of ourselves and the world."

Siobhan: (Engaged) "You're so right, Patrick. It's fascinating how travel can be both a journey outward and inward."

Patrick: (Thoughtful) "Speaking of journeys, have you ever considered taking up a new hobby? Sometimes trying something entirely different can be as enriching as exploring a new country."

Siobhan: (Reflective) "That's an interesting thought. Lately, I've been curious about learning to play the piano. The idea of creating music is both exciting and a bit intimidating."

Patrick: (Encouraging) "Learning to play an instrument is a rewarding challenge. I remember when I decided to learn how to cook. It felt daunting at first, but mastering a new recipe gives a similar sense of accomplishment."

Siobhan: (Curious) "Cooking is something I'd love to improve at too. Any favorite dish you're particularly proud of?"

Patrick: (Chuckles) "Well, I've managed to create a pretty mean lasagna recipe. It took a few tries, but now it's a go-to for family gatherings."

Siobhan: (Amused) "A homemade lasagna does sound impressive. It's interesting how our interests and passions can lead us down such diverse paths."

Patrick: (Engaged) "Absolutely, Siobhan. Talking about passions, have you ever thought about how experiences from your past shape your outlook on life today?"

Siobhan: (Thoughtful) "Definitely. Growing up, my family moved around quite a bit, and that exposed me to different cultures and perspectives. I believe it's why I'm so drawn to exploring new places now."

Patrick: (Intrigued) "It's amazing how childhood experiences can have such a lasting impact. For me, growing up with a strong sense of discipline due to my father's military background has shaped my approach to challenges."

Siobhan: (Curious) "That's really interesting, Patrick. How has that perspective influenced your decisions and experiences?"

Patrick: (Reflective) "It's taught me the importance of perseverance and adaptability. These traits have been valuable in my career and personal life, helping me navigate unexpected turns."

Siobhan: (Engaged) "Those are valuable life lessons. It's wonderful how our individual journeys lead us to who we are today."

Patrick: (Content) "Yes, our journeys are like a collection of puzzle pieces that come together to form a unique picture."

Note: In this dialogue, Patrick and Siobhan seamlessly transition from discussing travel to exploring hobbies and then delve into the impact of past experiences on their outlooks. The conversation flows naturally as they exchange insights and personal stories, and they conclude with a reflection on the way their life experiences have shaped them.

Remember, these strategies aren't rigid scripts – they're your toolkit for creating authentic connections. Adapt them to the flow of your conversations and the unique chemistry you share with each woman. By infusing your conversations with genuine interest and warmth, you're setting the stage for a connection that goes beyond the surface.

Q&A

Q: I find myself hesitant to employ the suggested flirting remarks. Is it possible to rely on my usual sense of humor to initiate playful conversations?
A: Certainly! When engaging with women, authenticity is key. Rather than imitating others, it's essential to express yourself naturally. The examples provided are intended to convey the essence of flirting, offering a guideline. Embrace your own humor, while also integrating subtle hints of your romantic interest during the initial exchange.
Q: Is it acceptable to bring up common subjects like weather, TV programs, or other people during small talk?
A: Certainly, you can include these topics, but remember that small talk with a woman you're interested in holds a different significance than a casual chat with friends or strangers. Rather than simply passing the time, aim to lay the groundwork for a more profound con-

nection. While introducing these everyday subjects is fine, avoid letting impersonal topics overpower the conversation.

Q: Can I forge a connection with women of all kinds?
A: Absolutely, you have the potential to connect with women from various backgrounds and personalities. However, there are two vital factors to take into account:

- ❑ **Shared Interest:** Building a connection relies on mutual interest. If she isn't inclined to engage in deeper conversations for whatever reason, the potential for establishing a connection could be limited.
- ❑ **Shared Values:** Moreover, compatibility is crucial. For instance, if your preferences diverge significantly – for instance, you have a preference against smokers and she happens to be a smoker, then investing in a meaningful connection might not be productive.

Q: Is forming a meaningful connection an essential prerequisite for entering into a relationship?
A: In most cases, it holds great importance. Nevertheless, there are instances, like those in a nightclub environment, where a hookup can occur following a superficial exchange. However, if this connection isn't deepened in subsequent interactions, the relationship could encounter hurdles. It's worth noting that relationships founded on superficial attributes like appearance or material possessions are at risk of encountering challenges and are less likely to endure over time.

Q: When's the optimal time to initiate in-depth conversations?
A: The timing is context-dependent. While there are no hard-and-fast rules, consider these pointers:

- ❑ **Setting and Comfort:** If the environment allows for focused interaction without too many distractions, you can embark on the journey of forming a meaningful connection. However, always ensure she's receptive to such discussions. Remember, building a connection is a gradual process spanning several interactions.

❏ **Early Phases of Dating:** If you've had a brief exchange and she's agreed to a date, it's appropriate to explore deeper conversation topics during your first outing.

❏ **Initial Contact:** It's worth noting that a profound connection isn't a prerequisite for obtaining her phone number or asking her out.

As you've gained insights into the art of engaging conversations, encompassing everything from flirtatious banter to meaningful connections, you're well-equipped to navigate the next step. In the upcoming chapters, we'll delve into the dynamic world of successful approaches in both real-life situations and dating apps. With these skills in your arsenal, you're well-prepared to embark on the exciting journey of effectively navigating various contexts and enhancing your dating experiences.

Chapter 3
FISHING IN UNCHARTED WATERS

1. Embrace the Approach: Triumph over Fear

Dear Journal,

Today was one of those days that I wish I could rewind and play over with a different script. There I was sitting in that quaint coffee shop nestled on the corner of a bustling street drinking my usual latte when my eyes caught her – a vision amidst the ordinary. She sat alone, bathed in sunlight, her gaze fixed on her phone as if she held the universe within it.

My heart raced, and I knew I had to talk to her. But alas, my tongue felt like it had suddenly turned to lead. I stood there, rehearsing possible openers in my mind, but each one felt either too cheesy or not clever enough. The fear of saying the wrong thing paralyzed me. What if my words stumbled and she laughed? Or worse, what if I accidentally offended her?

As time passed, I kept stealing glances in her direction, hoping to muster the courage to go over and say something. But every time I considered it, a wave of anxiety crashed over me. The battle between my desire to connect and my fear of rejection raged on, leaving me stuck in this frustrating limbo.

Lost in my thoughts, I failed to notice the seconds ticking by. And then, when I looked up, the table she occupied was empty. Just like that, she was gone.

I cursed my indecisiveness, my inability to seize the moment.

And so, I left the coffee shop, not with her number or a date, but with a strange mix of regret and resignation. I missed an opportunity to spark a conversation with her, and the "what ifs" are tormenting me. It's like I'm replaying a scene from a movie where the protagonist can't summon the words to speak to the one they admire most because he's afraid of losing her. Yes, I was afraid of losing her.

But wait! How can I lose something that I never had in the first place? The truth is, I built up this scenario in my mind without realizing that I have nothing to lose.

So, I suppose this is a lesson — a reminder that sometimes, we create our own heartaches by attaching ourselves to fears that may never come true. As I close this journal entry, I promise myself that next time, I'll seize the opportunity, come what may. After all, how can I truly lose something that was never mine to begin with?

Until next time,

The Same Old Me

Sound familiar? Oh, it does to me, big time. If I had kept a diary back in my teen days or when I was just stepping into the adult world, that journal would've been bursting with stories just like the one I've been talking about. I wasn't exactly Mr. Shy Guy – I could hold my own around girls, especially the ones I got to know through my friends. But when it came to chatting up girls who were total strangers, I'd go into full freeze mode.

The cool, confident dude in me? Yeah, he'd do a disappearing act, leaving behind a nervous, bumbling mess whenever I tried to strike up a convo with a girl, I'd never crossed paths with before. Let me tell you, this setup didn't exactly float my boat. It cramped my style big time. See, not every connection could happen through the usual gang, and sometimes, it'd be months before I stumbled upon a girlfriend through friends.

Using those dating sites everyone's talking about? Nah, they weren't my jam. Plus, those sites were mostly visited by folks older than me, which, you know, was a tad awkward for a young buck like me. So, the only card I had to play was talking to girls I'd never met before. But that? Well, it meant I had to kick that "deer in head-lights" feeling that kept me from moving forward in the romance game.

Now, when you're trying to sort out a problem, you've got to pinpoint what's causing the glitch before you can fix it, right? So, I figured out that my prime stumbling block was the sheer terror of things not going as planned. Crazy, right? It's like skipping a job interview because you're afraid you won't get the gig. Silly stuff! But you know what? This little fear bug is what gets most guys all jittery. It's like their brain feeds on a diet of bad movie scripts, and eventually, they start thinking that making a move is totally uncool, or that only the rich or the handsome hit the jackpot, which is not always the case.

Indeed, wealthy and good-looking individuals may have a distinct advantage, but that doesn't imply that those who haven't been blessed by nature with remarkable physiques or don't reside in opulent mansions are destined for loneliness. With the right attitude, anyone can score.

In my quest to crush this fear of failure, I remembered three life rules that have always had my back:

🖹 Embrace the Action: "Just Do It"

The iconic Nike slogan, "Just Do It," became my trusty companion as I navigated the trials and tribulations of childhood. From scaling trees to daring leaps between buildings, this mantra emboldened me to conquer the audacious escapades that demanded a brave heart. But here's the kicker – it wasn't just about physical feats. This motto stood strong when I had to muster the courage to invite a classmate to dance or take that leap into a first kiss.

It was as if those three simple words held a magical power, in-fusing me with the determination to breach the boundaries of my comfort zone. "Just Do It" whispered courage into my ear every time I teetered on the edge of hesitation. And guess what? The irony is delightful – I never even sported a pair of Nike shoes.

📝 The "So What" Mindset

Will she give you the cold shoulder when you make your move? So what? The "so what" attitude is your ultimate shield when it's time to step up and approach a girl. Picture it like this: approaching is a game, and if she's not up for a match, that's on her. And guess what? It doesn't need to dent your confidence, not even if her re-sponse comes with a side of frost. When it comes to making con-nections, and life in general, having the knack for not taking things overly seriously is an ace in the hole.

Remember those times when someone tried to ruffle your feath-ers with a snide comment, leaving you temporarily lost for words? We've all been there. Now, here's the magical thing I've learned: in those moments, a nonchalant "So What" is the perfect comeback. It's like a verbal mic drop that stops their show. You see, by refusing to give them the satisfaction of a reaction, you foil their game plan, leaving them high and dry.

Now, let's translate this to approaching. Imagine you strut up to a girl with a line you've got all figured out, and she comes back with, "That's the best you've got?" or "Seriously, that's your line?" Don't sweat it. A cool-as-a-cucumber "Yes, so what? You're talking to me now, aren't you?" or "Why does it matter?" sends a powerful mes-sage – you're not here to jump through hoops for her amusement. This attitude doesn't just disarm her challenges; it empowers you.

Think about it – when you embrace the "So What" approach, you're not just mastering the art of charm; you're mastering life it-self. And trust me, the girl who witnesses you navigate these mo-ments with a carefree attitude will have a hard time resisting your magnetic confidence. So, whether you're in the realm of seduction or just tackling the everyday hustle, remember the "So What" mindset – it's your secret weapon for success.

You Have Nothing to Lose: Grasp Those Chances

In my epic showdown with the fear of floundering, a pesky thought squirmed in my mind: "What if my approach ends in a girl-shaped disaster?" It hovered there until I realized something huge – how can you lose something you didn't have to begin with? It's like worrying about losing the lottery ticket you never bought. You see where I'm going with this, right?

Here's the enlightenment that struck me: if I didn't take the plunge and approach, absolutely zilch would happen. She'd vanish into the universe, never to grace my life again. So technically, I'd be batting zero. But! On the flip side, mustering the courage to make a move could lead to an epic love story. Even if my opening line earned me a rejection, what's the damage? I began with zero, remember?

So, let me take you back to when I was 12, and I decided to invite a girl I barely knew to my birthday party.

I had recently noticed a girl named Emily in my school. We had exchanged a few words here and there, but we were light years from being friends. My birthday was approaching, and a wild idea crossed my mind. I decided to take a leap of faith and invite her to my birthday party. The fear of turning that simple invitation into a catastrophe was real. But it was almost as if life whispered, "Why not give it a shot? What do you have to lose?"

So, with a touch of nervous excitement, I approached Emily one day after school. "Hey, Emily," I said, "I'm having a birthday party this weekend, and I'd like to invite you. It would be great if you could make it."

Emily hesitated for a moment, and my heart raced. Then, with a warm smile, she said, "Sure, I'd love to come!"

Emily came to my birthday party, and we had a fantastic time.

Looking back, I realized that my fear of inviting her almost held me back from experiencing the joy of her company. But thanks to the "You Have Nothing to Lose" ethos I now hold dear, I took a chance that marked the beginning of my romantic adventures.

Now, I know that approaching a girl at the age of 12 in a schoolyard is not the same as approaching a woman in a coffee shop as an adult, but is the same fear.

So, my compadres, as you stand at the crossroads of approaching those enigmatic strangers, etch this rule deep into your psyche. It's not just about initiating conversations; it's about confidently diving into the unknown, seizing the chances life throws your way, and showing yourself that the greatest failure lies in never daring at all. Will every approach lead to fireworks? Not necessarily. But remember, each time you embrace an opportunity, you're already creating something remarkable in the story of your life.

Yet, acknowledging that approaching is a universal challenge, I've curated a collection of guidelines to infuse your approach journey with ease and delight. Join me as we delve into the treasure trove of these practices.

First, we will discuss the factors that make an approach less prone to rejection, we will explore various icebreakers along with a few approach examples, and how to wrap up the interaction, leaving you with her number.

2. Approaches Key Points

✎ Approach Selectively

Now, I get it. It's tempting to want to dive into the vast sea of opportunities and meet every fish in the dating pond. But hold your seahorses! Just because there's a buffet doesn't mean you have to munch on every dish. Remember that "selective" isn't just a setting on your streaming service; it's a golden rule.

If you've taken my advice and crafted that nifty checklist I raved about earlier, you're already ahead in the game. Picture this: your mental mood board showcasing the kind of girl who resonates with your wavelength. We're talking about those visual cues – the makeup, the style, the whole vibe. Mind you, this isn't a Sherlock-level deduction about her favorite movie genres just yet.

Let's say you're a connoisseur of sophistication, magnetically drawn to girls who ooze grace from every pore. But wait, here comes a wild card – a girl who's practically a neon sign of "anything goes," radiating vulgarity. Now, before you whip out your wingman cape, pause and ponder. Is it worth it? This isn't just a numbers game; it's about quality over quantity.

Before you take that leap of faith, engage in a little tête-à-tête with your inner chatterbox. Ask yourself, "Would I enjoy a tête-à-tête with this girl?" And, just for kicks, "Could I picture her hilariously squirming at a family dinner?"

Now, here's the deal. Chatting up with someone who resonates with your jam is like wearing your favorite socks – super comfy. It sets the stage for breezy conversations, and trust me, that's where the magic happens. So, put that selective swag on, and watch your approach become a runway for success.

⌑ Lock Eyes, Say Hi

Remember that moment when you caught eyes with someone across the room? Those milliseconds that felt like an eternity, a secret code shared amidst the bustling crowd? Well, that's the magic of eye contact, my friend – the silent symphony of curiosity, intrigue, and maybe a hint of attraction. And guess what? It's not just the warm-up; it's the opening act of a potentially great show.

As I spilled the beans in the latter part of our initial tête-à-tête, eye contact is your unsung hero, signaling that a girl might just be on the same wavelength. It's like a cosmic nod that says, "Hey, you, over there. You're kinda interesting." A prolonged gaze? Well, that's practically the universe sending you an engraved invitation to the dance.

Now, picture this: you've locked eyes with someone who's triggered that flutter in your stomach. Your heart skips a beat or two – maybe more, no judgment here. It's as if a light bulb pinged on over both your heads. That's your cue, my friend. The universe just handed you a sparkly baton, and it's time to run with it.

So, here's the kicker. If the universe is offering you a backstage pass, are you going to decline? I didn't think so. Approach the girl who shared that clandestine eye code with you. It's not just an approach; it's a continuation of that silent conversation that began with a glance.

It's like the universe left you a voice note that says, "Hey, you've got potential here. Don't let it fizzle out." And who are you to argue with the universe? So, seize the cosmic connection, walk over with confidence, and remember, my friend, you're not just approaching. You're picking up where the stars left off.

⚷ Go for the Yawns

Alright, time to tackle a scenario that might seem straight out of a classic rom-com – approaching the "bored beauties." These are usually the solo players on the dating field, the ones who, let's be honest, haven't found a dancing partner for life just yet. And guess what? Boredom often becomes their unexpected plus one.

So, let's paint the scene. You're at an event, scanning the crowd like the undercover cupid you are. And there they are – groups of girls, chatting away and looking like they're out for a friendly soirée. But wait, there's a telltale sign. In a cluster of giggles and gossip, you spot the lone ranger. The third wheel. The one who's not exactly jiving with the conversation or showing off her dance moves.

Now, before you think, "Oh no, the party's a drag," let me sprinkle some magic on this scenario. You see, these "bored beauties" aren't just wallflowers; they're potential conversation goldmines. Why? Because in a sea of chatter and camaraderie, they might just be the hidden treasure waiting for the right explorer to come along.

Imagine this: a trio of two girls and a guy. The girls are in sync, talking and twirling with the guy. But what about the extra gal? Chances are, she's standing there, twiddling her thumbs, her eyes wandering. Why? Well, her pals are in a dynamic duo, and she's feeling more like a "spectator" than a "participant". That's your cue, my friend.

Approaching the "bored beauties" is like entering a portal of possibility. It's the unexpected twist in the story of connections. Think about it – while others might shy away from the girl who's seemingly uninvolved, you're stepping into the scene like the charming lead who's here to shake things up.

So, next time you spot a solo star in a galaxy of giggles, don't think "blah." Think "bold." Think "opportunity." Think "I'm the guy who can make her laugh, dance, and forget about being the third wheel."

Now, go be the cure to their "yawn" and turn it into a "yarn" of a tale that starts with a "Hey, are you up for a non-boring conversation?" Because sometimes, the unexpected "plus one" can turn out to be the most delightful surprise.

ꙮ Friendliness First

Alright, let's talk about how to make sure you're playing the approach game on "easy mode." Now, I don't have an inside scoop on your personal "girl vibes" preference, but here's a nifty nugget: until you've honed your approach skills, it's like dipping your toes in the water first. You'd rather sidestep the ones who are sending off vibes of "Queen Bee" or "I'm-not-here-to-mingle." Trust me, these ones are like the spicy hot sauce of the dating world – they can leave you a bit tongue-tied.

Picture this: you've got your approach mojo on, you're ready to swoop in with charisma, and then bam! You land in a conversation with someone who could give even the most seasoned debaters a run for their money. These are the "scorpions" of the dating jungle, armed with quips that might leave you doing the conversational cha-cha.

Here's where the plot twist comes in. While it's tempting to dive into the deep end right away, remember that even the most epic adventures start with a few warm-up exercises. This is the stage where you want to spot the friendly faces, the ones who've got "approachable" written all over them.

You're looking for those who don't just light up a room; they light up conversations too. The ones whose laughter feels like a melody you want to hum along to. These are the "easy mode" players in the dating game. Approach them, and you're likely to find yourself in a chat that flows like a lazy river on a summer's day.

And hey, I get it – life sometimes throws curveballs. You might unexpectedly find yourself in a chat with someone who seems to have a Ph.D. in "conversation combat." That's when you whip out the "So What" attitude. Remember, every interaction is a learning experience, and sometimes even the toughest ones can be transformed into tales of triumph.

So, whether you're sipping on a conversational cappuccino with the "easy mode" champs or tangling with the "scorpions," keep your "So What" card handy. With the right mix of friendly vibes and a pinch of attitude, you'll be a master at this game in no time.

☞ Dance Floor 101

Ready to dive into the dance floor dynamics? Let's do this! Imagine you're in the heart of the dance party, surrounded by the electric energy of friends and music. You're grooving like nobody's watching, and here's a little secret – someone is.

Enter the dance floor magnetism. As you and your friends create your own dance universe, you become a charismatic center of gravity, attracting eyes like a moth to a flame. The girls in the room — eyes like hawks – notice your aura of fun and confidence.

And guess what? If their dance moves are a secret Morse code for "let's connect," they're about as subtle as a neon sign. If they're looking to mingle, they'll pull off the classic "dance-close-but-not-too-close" maneuver. Translation: they're shimmying into your orbit, hoping to be noticed, hoping for a connection.

Here's where the plot thickens: you might not find them boldly marching over with a "Hi, let's chat." But you know what's up? Those dance steps are practically Morse code for "Hey, I'm here, make a move if you dare."

It's like a scene out of a rom-com, where the universe aligns the dance moves, and you're the lead actor in this script. So, while they might not throw the first conversational punch, they've definitely set the stage for a chat that could rival any dance-off.

Bottom line: the dance floor isn't just for shaking off the stress; it's a playground of opportunities. Embrace the power of the dance, embrace the magnetic pull, and trust your gut. If her dance moves are inching closer to yours, consider it your invitation to waltz into her world.

Remember, when the dance moves are aligned, the only thing left to do is spin the conversation into motion. So, let the dance of words begin, and who knows? This could be the start of a beautiful partnership – both on and off the dance floor.

⌐ Approach with Confident Charisma

Ready to rock the approach? Let's talk about how to strut onto the scene with confidence and magnetic energy. Because guess what? Your attitude is the golden ticket to creating an inviting atmosphere that she won't be able to resist.

Imagine this: you're strolling up to her with an air of self-assuredness, and your positive energy is practically sparking in the air. It's like stepping onto a stage where you're the star of the show, and she's the intrigued audience waiting for your performance.

Now, let's steer clear of the gloom and doom territory. Approaching with a nervous demeanor is like bringing a rain cloud to a sunny day – it dampens the mood. And you know what happens when she feels uncomfortable? She might not be in the mood for a conversation rollercoaster.

But here's the secret sauce: your vibes shape your approach. A gloomy attitude sends a message she might not want to receive. On the other hand, radiating relaxation and positivity sets the stage for a lively conversation. It's like you're passing her a virtual "Welcome" drink, inviting her to relax and enjoy the interaction.

As you step forward, it's time to dial up the charm. Confidence? Check. Sociability? Double check. Wit? You've got it. It's like you've walked onto a stage, and you're the charismatic lead who's about to sweep her off her feet.

And remember, when you're comfortable in your own skin, she's more likely to feel at ease too. Your positive energy becomes a dance, a rhythm that she can't help but groove to.

So, before you approach, remind yourself: you're not just a bystander in this interaction; you're the conductor of your own symphony. Confidence is your crescendo, and positive vibes are your harmony. With this winning combo, you're not just approaching – you're making a magnetic entrance into a world of endless possibilities.

☞ Embrace the Art of Spontaneity

Ready to unleash the magic of spontaneous conversation? Let's dive into the world of approaching without a moment's hesitation. Here's the scoop: spontaneity is your wingman in this game, and mastering it is your secret weapon.

Now, here's where most guys stumble – a hesitation that's like putting a fork in the road and never choosing a direction. They wait, and they wait some more until they're finally ready to strike up a conversation. But by then, the atmosphere might be like stale bread, leaving her to wonder if you've got better things to do.

Here's the truth bomb: Women adore confidence and spontaneity. What they're not fans of? The whole "stalker vibes" thing. Circling around like a curious cat, staring without end – yeah, that's not winning you any points.

In the grand game of approaching, timing is your sidekick. Act fast, because your brain is like a trickster who either comes up with a hundred excuses not to approach or starts crafting that "perfect" line, which, let's face it, might just be too little too late.

Remember, spontaneity is like the secret spice that gives your approach that extra kick. So, let's kick off the journey into the art of striking up conversations with girls you haven't met before, the ones who haven't come knocking through familiar doors.

3. Cracking the Ice: Approaches in Everyday Encounters

Alright, let's dive into the secret sauce of making an approach that's as smooth as butter... or as smooth as butter can be in those heart-pounding moments. And here's the golden nugget: It's not all about the perfect opening line. Nope, it's not about having an "icebreaker" so genius that it'd make even the greatest pickup guru jealous. Nope, not at all. Because here's the kicker – if the stars aren't aligning or the mood isn't right, even the wittiest line won't turn the tides.

Picture this: You're in the arena, ready for action, but your opponent isn't playing ball. Maybe they're already on the relationship rollercoaster, or they're vibing with a different playlist, or perhaps they're simply not into conversing with random strangers (it's a real thing, folks!). Or, and bear with me, they might just not see you as the hero they've been waiting for. And that's perfectly fine – because guess what? It's all part of the game. Our job as guys? We're here to roll the dice, take a chance, and embrace the unpredictability.

So, you spot a face that has your heart doing the cha-cha, and you decide to roll those dice. Here's the lowdown on making it work:

The Rule of "Hi"

No, it's not an official rule – it's more like a sly trick from the Book of Social Shenanigans. Start with a casual "Hi," and then hit the pause button. Observe her reaction – is she pulling a face like she just bit into a lemon, or is she staring at you like you're a unicorn? If it's the unicorn stare, you're on track to strike up a chat. But hey, if she looks like she'd rather be anywhere else, no worries. Just tell her you were talking to the elevator and shuffle away. If the stars twinkle in your favor, continue with your next move. Now, not every chat has to kick off with a greeting but hey, it's comforting to realize you've got the superpower to predict potential awkwardness from just a simple "Hi!" Trust me, the "Hi" radar is real!

The Rule of No Logic

Think of this as your VIP ticket to Banterland. An icebreaker doesn't have to make logical sense; in fact, the more whimsical, the better. Picture this: "Guess who's secretly a superhero in this room?" Now, I know what you're thinking – superheroes in real life? Nah, but that's the beauty. This might prompt her to respond with something equally humorous, and voila – you've got yourself a giggly convo.

Women enjoy playful conversations, but to achieve that, the interaction needs to start playfully. Starting with a formal or serious opener may lead to a similarly serious response, limiting the conversation's potential. Instead, why not throw in a curveball of absurdity that leaves her smiling and intrigued? It's like showing up to a costume party in an astronaut suit – women are drawn to the unexpected. So, if you ever catch yourself contemplating a mundane opener, consider switching gears and embracing the wacky side of life. Remember, it's all about sparking her curiosity with the element of surprise.

The Rule of Context

We're talking about a tag team here, where your opener and the scene play nice. Imagine this: you're in the elevator, and time's ticking slower than molasses. You hit her with the question, "Have you ever wondered why elevators are slower than sloths?" She might respond with a "No idea," and bam – you're the guy with the answer: "Neither do I, but I heard that if you chat about elevators with a random soul in an elevator, you'll have the raddest day ever." See, it's like social magic or something.

The Rule of Comfort

Your opener should be delivered with a sprinkle of friendliness and a dash of charm. The goal? A chill, no-pressure vibe that makes her feel like you're two people on the same wavelength, not an interrogation squad. Remember, it's all about keeping it breezy and delightful, no matter which way the chat goes.

But wait, theory's over – let's dive into the treasure trove of real-world openers. I've sorted them into two blockbuster categories: "Daytime Settings" (think parks, cafes, shops, and buses) and "Nightlife Settings" (cue the club lights and dance floors). Plus,

144

we've got a few wildcards that fit both zones – because hey, versatility is the name of the game.

So, put on your charm cap, make these openers your own, and get ready to level up your banter game. It's time to turn those chance encounters into unforgettable stories.

① Daytime Settings

☕ Icebreakers for Coffee Shop Settings

Enter the world of coffee shops, where the aroma of fresh brews mingles with the possibility of new connections. Whether it's a quaint corner café or a bustling urban espresso bar, coffee shops offer a unique space for encounters. If you spot a woman sitting solo at a table, don't let the chance slip away. With these icebreakers tailored for coffee shop settings, you'll be sipping on stimulating conversations in no time. Plus, feel free to adapt these icebreakers for similar settings or when she's enjoying a different beverage.

- 🗨 "Mind if I intrude on your solo coffee symphony? I heard two is the new one when it comes to enjoying coffee vibes."
- 🗨 "I'm on a mission to combat the terrible loneliness that strikes when one sits solo at a table. Care to join my noble cause?"
- 🗨 "I have this theory that coffee gets jealous when you're sitting alone, so it starts losing its flavor. Mind if I rescue both you and your coffee from a potential taste crisis?"
- 🗨 "I just realized my coffee looks lonely over there. Mind if I introduce it to your coffee and see if they hit it off?"
- 🗨 "Pardon the intrusion, but my coffee and I have been having a heated debate about whether tables are meant for one or two. Would you mind being the tiebreaker?"
- 🗨 "Excuse me, but I couldn't help noticing that your table

seems to have a vacancy for one witty conversation partner. Mind if I apply for the position?"

- "I've been receiving distress signals from my coffee that it's feeling isolated. Would you mind if I brought it over for a coffee support group meeting?"
- "I've heard that coffee beans whisper secrets to those who enjoy them in pairs. Care to join my coffee espionage mission?"
- "Rumor has it that the coffee here stages a protest when it sees someone sitting solo. Mind if I join your coffee protest alliance?"
- "Excuse me, but do you believe in the coffee shop fairy tales? You know, the ones where two strangers share a table and end up having hilarious conversations?"

🗪 Example of an approach in a coffee shop:

Setting: Eric and Hanna find themselves in a cozy coffee shop with the aroma of freshly brewed coffee in the air. Hanna is sitting alone at a small table, sipping on her latte and enjoying a quiet moment.

Eric: (Friendly) "Hi!"
Hanna: (Smiling) "Hi!"
Eric: (Playfully) "I have this theory that coffee tastes better when you're not sitting alone at the table. Mind if I Join You?"
Hanna: (Amused) "Sure, go ahead."
Eric: (Smiling) "Thanks! I'm Eric, by the way. Just thought I'd introduce myself properly after crashing your solo coffee session."
Hanna: (Nodding) "Nice to meet you, Eric. I'm Hanna. Thanks for asking before sitting down. It's not every day someone actually bothers with manners."
Eric: (Chuckles) "Well, manners go a long way, don't they? Plus,

I've had my fair share of awkward coffee shop encounters, so I figured starting with a little politeness might lead to a less cringe-worthy conversation."

Hanna: (Laughs) "I can relate to that. So, what's the worst coffee shop encounter you've had?"

Eric: (Smirking) "Oh, the time I mistook someone else's drink for mine and ended up sipping a caramel macchiato when I'm strictly a black coffee guy. It was like a betrayal to my coffee beliefs."

Hanna: (Laughs) "That's quite the coffee drama. I'm more of a latte person myself, but I can imagine the shock."

Eric: (Playfully) "So, Hanna, aside from talking with strangers in coffee shops, what other secret passions do you have?"

Note: In this dialog, Eric, intrigued by Hanna's presence, playfully approaches her with a theory about coffee tasting better when shared. Hanna, amused by his approach, allows him to join her. They exchange introductions, with Eric emphasizing the importance of manners in such encounters. Their conversation revolves around their coffee preferences and a humorous coffee shop mishap, leading to a lighthearted exchange. The dialog highlights Eric's playful and engaging approach, creating a relaxed atmosphere for their conversation and fostering a potential connection.

🏋️ Icebreakers for Gym Settings

Among the clank of weights and the rhythm of cardio, opportunities to strike up conversations abound. Whether you're pumping iron or hitting the treadmill, these icebreakers will help you break a sweat and break the ice. Let's turn those reps into conversations and make your workout sessions even more rewarding!

- "Hi! Mind if I interrupt your workout for a quick gym-related question?"

- "Hi there! You seem to be acing your workout game. Any pro tips for a fellow gym enthusiast?"
- "Hey! I couldn't help but notice your impressive form. Are you secretly a fitness guru in disguise?"
- "Hi! I'm on a mission to crack the mysteries of gym motivation. Any chance you're a motivational wizard?"
- "Hey! I hope you don't mind me saying this, but your gym vibe is seriously motivating. What's your secret?"
- "Hi there! I'm trying to solve the puzzle of finding the perfect workout routine. Any chance you've got a few pieces to share?"
- "Hey! Your energy in here is contagious. Do you have a secret stash of gym motivation that you're willing to share?"
- "Hi! I've been wondering, Do you have a secret superhero gym routine? Your dedication is seriously impressive!"
- "Hey there! I'm in awe of your gym game. Got any workout hacks that you're willing to pass on?"
- "Hi! I must say, your dedication is catching my attention. Care to share a fitness tidbit with a fellow gym-goer?"

🗨 Example of an approach at the gym:

Setting: In a bustling and well-equipped gym, where the clinking of weights and the soft hum of treadmills fill the air, Caleb spots Olivia busy conquering exercise machines. Caleb decides to make his move, approaching Olivia with a friendly demeanor.

Caleb: (Friendly) "Hi there."
Olivia: (Smiling) "Hi."
Caleb: (Curious) "Mind if I interrupt your equipment conquering for a quick question?"
Olivia: (Amused) "Depends on the question, I guess."
Caleb: (Playful) "Can you help me unlock the mysteries of this machine?"

Olivia: (Laughs) "Well, I'll do my best to be your equipment sensei. What's puzzling you?"

Caleb: (Grinning) "I've been staring at this thing, trying to figure out its secrets, but it's resisting all my charm. I think it's secretly mocking me."

Olivia: (Chuckling) "Ah, the ancient equipment riddle. I see what's going on. You just need to speak its language. And by that, I mean adjust the tension here and the angle there."

Caleb: (Acting impressed) "The language of weights and pulleys, I should've known! I owe you for saving me from my own confusion. I'm Caleb, by the way."

Olivia: (Smiling) "Nice to meet you Caleb, I'm Olivia."

Caleb: (Playful) "So, Olivia, what do you up to when you are not helping strangers unlock equipment mysteries?"

Note: As Caleb approaches Olivia in the gym, he seeks her help in understanding the exercise machine. Olivia, with a touch of humor, plays the role of "equipment sensei." She gives him some guidance, and they exchange introductions. This initial interaction, sparked by Caleb's playful approach, opens the door to further conversation and the potential for a budding connection.

🛒 Icebreakers for Shopping Center Settings

Step into the vibrant world of shopping centers, where people bustle and bags rustle. Amidst the aisles of retail therapy, conversations can bloom just like a fresh find. Join me as we dive into icebreakers tailored for shopping center settings. Whether you're browsing for deals or exploring with intent, these icebreakers will add a touch of social zest to your shopping expedition. Let's navigate the lanes of connection and discovery together!

Clothing Store:

- "Hey, quick vote! Does this shirt scream 'weekend adventurer' or 'urban explorer' to you?"
- "I've got a fashion dilemma: Should I rock the superhero vibes with this jacket or unleash my inner rockstar?"
- "I'm on a quest for the perfect outfit that says 'confident risk-taker.' Would you recommend the daring or the dashing?"
- "Do you think this scarf gives off a 'mysterious spy on vacation' vibe, or more of a 'fearless explorer at a tea party' feel?"
- "Excuse me, I could use a second opinion. Which of these suits do you think would make a stronger impression at an important event?"
- "I'm shopping for a special occasion, and I'm torn between a classic look and something a bit more adventurous. What's your style advice?"
- "I'm on the hunt for a shirt that strikes the perfect balance between casual and stylish. Any recommendations?"

Electronics Store:

- "I need a gadget that's as impressive as my heroic dance moves. Any recommendations for something that'll catch both eyes and hearts?"
- "Between these devices, which one do you think will help me level up in real life?"
- "I'm on a mission to find a tech sidekick that matches my charismatic energy. Which gadget here can keep up with my charm?"
- "Hey there, I'm on a mission to find the perfect gadget. Any recommendations for something that'll impress both humans and aliens?"
- "I'm on the hunt for a device that's not just cutting-edge but also has a touch of futuristic appeal. Any ideas on what

might fit the bill?"

- "Excuse me, I'm on the lookout for a device that adds a little 'wow' factor to my tech collection. Any recommendations that combine style and functionality?"

Toy Store:

- "You know, I might be an adult, but my curiosity levels are still off the charts. Which toy do you think could satisfy my itch for adventure?"
- "I'm all about grown-up responsibilities, but deep down, I'm still a kid. Which toy here screams 'bring out the inner child'?"
- "I'm convinced that toys are the key to world peace. Which one can bridge the gap between fun and world-saving strategy?"
- "I've been searching for the ultimate board game for legendary game nights. Which one here is rumored to have a secret passage to Candyland?"
- "Hey, I'm searching for the perfect toy that's both nostalgic and entertaining. Any favorites you'd recommend for a trip down memory lane?"
- "Excuse me, I'm on a mission to find a fun and unique toy. Any recommendations for a [child age and gender]?"

Sporting Goods:

- "Confession: I'm more of a thinker than an athlete, but I want to dive into the world of sports. Any recommendations for a sport that suits a mind in motion?"
- "Let's be real, I'm all about strategizing, but I need sportswear that can handle my 'sudden dance party' moves. Any suggestions?"
- "I'm on a quest to find the sport that combines intellectual

prowess with strategic agility. What's your bet on the perfect match?"

🔊 "I've heard that wearing the right shoes can improve your chances of winning at rock-paper-scissors. Any shoe here that specializes in 'rock'?"

🔊 "Hey, I'm looking to up my game in [mention a sport]. Any suggestions on gear or accessories that can give me an edge?"

🔊 "Hi there! I'm in the market for some new sports equipment. Any recommendations for must-have items?"

Jewelry Store:

🔊 "I've heard jewelry can hold secret powers. Which piece do you think can help me find my keys faster or make my coffee taste better?"

🔊 "Between these rings, which one do you think radiates 'magnetic charisma'?"

🔊 "I'm convinced the right piece of jewelry can channel my inner superhero. Which one do you think holds the power of 'charming conversations'?"

🔊 "I heard that wearing a certain ring can give you the ability to find the best parking spots. Any chance you can help me find that ring?"

🔊 "Hi there! I can't decide between 'subtle elegance' or 'shining disco ball.' Any advice for a confused shopper?"

Home Decor:

🔊 "My living space is my castle, and I want it to have a touch of magic. Which home item here would make Merlin jealous?"

🔊 "I'm on a quest to make my place the ultimate hangout spot.

Any item here that screams 'epic game nights and movie marathons'?"

🗩 "If my home could have a theme song, it'd be epic. Which decor piece can make it feel like the hero's triumphant return?"

🗩 "I've been told that the right lampshade can turn any room into a disco wonderland. Which one here has the most boogie potential?"

🗩 "Hey, I'm searching for that one quirky decor piece that'll leave guests asking, 'Where did you find this?' Any ideas?"

🗩 "Excuse me, I'm lost in this wonderland of home decor. Any recommendations for items that can make my home look like a magazine cover without breaking the bank?"

Shoe Store:

🗩 "Shoes can totally shape your destiny, right? Which pair here gives off the vibe of a dance floor superstar?"

🗩 "I need shoes that can handle both sprinting to catch the train and impressing in a spontaneous dance-off. Which one's screams 'multitasking marvel'?"

🗩 "I've heard that the right shoes can turn a regular day into a legendary one. Which pair here is known for its power of transformation?"

🗩 "I'm convinced that shoes have secret magical properties. Which pair do you think would grant me the power to dance like no one's watching?"

🗩 "Excuse me, I'm on a quest to find the perfect pair of shoes that will make me feel like I'm walking on clouds. Any recommendations for shoes that are as comfy as a marshmallow mattress?"

🗩 "Hi there! It looks like you have a great eye for shoes. What's the secret formula for finding shoes that look great and feel fantastic?"

Grocery Section:

- "My cooking skills might need some magic. Any ingredients here known for turning average meals into legendary feasts?"
- "I've heard that adding a certain spice can make conversations more enchanting. Which one do you think enhances storytelling?"
- "Between these culinary choices, which one can make my dishes taste as adventurous as they look?"
- "If one of these spices could unlock the ability to predict the weather, which one do you think Mother Nature prefers?"
- "Excuse me, I'm attempting to turn my shopping cart into a foodie's paradise. Any recommendations for items that can turn my kitchen into a gourmet restaurant?"

Home Improvement Section:

- "I'm trying to turn my home into a wizard's den. Any suggestions for furniture that can double as secret passageways or magical creature hangouts?"
- "Between these doormats, which one is rumored to welcome luck, lost treasures, and unexpected friendships?"
- "I've heard that having a magical doormat can bring good fortune. Which one here is known for granting wishes and finding lost socks?"
- "My home improvement goal is to create an ambiance that'll, make the knights of the Round Table jealous. Which piece here can transport me to the age of chivalry?"
- "Between these curtains, which one is known to keep out not only sunlight but also the temptation to take a cozy afternoon nap?"

Bookstore:

- "I'm on the hunt for a book that'll make me believe in time travel. Any recommendations for stories that can teleport me straight into history?"
- "Do you think books have secret alliances with coffee? Which one here promises the most epic reading experience with a side of caffeine?"
- "I'm searching for a novel that can challenge my imagination to a duel. Which book do you think would be my worthy opponent?"
- "I've heard reading is the closest thing to a magic spell. If I could only choose one enchanting tome, which one should I reach for?"
- "Hey, I'm looking for a book that's known to create a 'book hangover' effect. Any titles here that are guilty of keeping readers up all night?"
- "Hi! I'm looking for a book that makes me question the meaning of life. Any recommendations?"
- "Hi there! I'm on a quest to find a book that's so gripping it'll make me miss my bus stop. Any recommendations for a real page-turner?"

🗨 Example of an approach in a clothing store:

Setting: A fashionable clothing store in a bustling shopping mall. Henry approaches Amelia, who is looking at some clothing racks.

Henry: (Playfully) "Hey, quick vote! Does this shirt scream 'weekend adventurer' or 'urban explorer' to you?"
Amelia: (Smiling) "Oh, that's a tough one. I'd say it leans more towards 'weekend adventurer' with a hint of 'urban explorer' vibe."
Henry: (Grinning) "That's what I was thinking too! Thanks for

the input. By the way, I'm Henry."

Amelia: (Friendly) "Nice to meet you, Henry. I'm Amelia."

Henry: "So, Amelia, are you here shopping for something special, or just enjoying the fashion spectacle?"

Amelia: (Laughing) "A bit of both, actually. I'm looking for a dress for a friend's upcoming wedding, but I can't resist checking out the latest trends."

Henry: (Smiling) "Ah, weddings can be tricky. I'm sure you'll find the perfect dress. Any specific style in mind?"

Amelia: (Thoughtful) "I'm thinking something elegant but not too formal, you know? What about you? What brings you here today?"

Henry: (Chuckles) "Just exploring, really. I don't mind getting lost in the world of clothes. Any fashion tips for a fellow explorer like me?"

Amelia: (Playfully) "Always follow your fashion instincts. Sometimes the best discoveries happen when you trust your gut."

Henry: (Laughs) "I'll keep that in mind. So, tell me, Amelia, aside from giving fashion tips to strangers, what else fills your days?"

Note: Henry initiates the interaction with a playful question about a shirt, which serves as an excellent icebreaker. Amelia's response is engaging and allows them to connect over their shared perspective on the shirt. Henry then smoothly transitions to introductions, and the conversation naturally evolves to discussing their purposes for being in the clothing store. The final question about what fills Amelia's days is a natural way to delve into her interests, making it a good approach to building a connection with her. Overall, the approach is effective in creating a comfortable and engaging atmosphere for conversation.

📖 Icebreakers for Library Settings

Welcome to the library – a realm of quiet pages and thoughtful contemplation. But guess what? Even in this tranquil space, conversations can spark like ideas in the minds of readers. Here, we'll delve into icebreakers designed for library settings. Whether you're aiming to meet someone new or add a dash of sociable flair to your reading routine, these icebreakers are here to help.

- 🗨 "Do you believe in the library's secret magic? I'm convinced the books conspire to switch places when we're not looking."
- 🗨 "Excuse me, I'm on a quest for the ultimate book recommendation. Any chance you can help me decipher this ancient text of 'bestsellers'?"
- 🗨 "Is it just me, or does the library feel like a treasure hunt where the prize is a cozy reading nook?"
- 🗨 "Confession time: I'm on a mission to find the most comfortable chair for hours of uninterrupted reading. Any leads?"
- 🗨 "Can you settle a bet for me? My friend thinks the library is only for serious scholars, but I believe it's a realm of endless adventures. What's your take?"
- 🗨 "I have a theory that librarians are modern-day wizards who know every book's secret spell. What's your take on their mystical powers?"
- 🗨 "I've been pondering a philosophical question: Do fictional characters secretly meet up in the library after hours? What do you think?"
- 🗨 "You seem like you have the advanced course in library navigation. Any pro tips for a fellow explorer in search of the perfect reading corner?"

🐾 Example of an approach in a library:

Setting: A university library during midterm exams week. The library is packed with students studying for their exams, and there's a subtle sense of chaos as people search for available study spots.

Lucas: (Grinning) "You know, I always thought libraries were places of tranquility and serenity. But I just witnessed the most intense battle over the last available study desk."

Charlotte: (Chuckling) "Oh, believe me, the study desk wars are a real thing here. It's like a competitive sport sometimes."

Lucas: (Laughing) "Have you ever seen students give each other the evil eye for a quiet corner?"

Charlotte: (Amused) "Absolutely, I've seen 'the look' exchanged a few times. It's all part of the library survival strategy."

Lucas: (Smirking) "Library survival strategy, huh? I might need a crash course. I'm Lucas, by the way."

Charlotte: (Smiling) "I'm Charlotte"

Lucas: (playful) "Nice to meet you, Charlotte. So, what else should I know about this library?"

Charlotte: (Smiling) "Well, we have a secret society of book nerds who meet in the shadows to discuss plot twists."

Lucas: (Playful) "Ah, the clandestine world of literary conspiracies. I must be initiated. Anything else I should be aware of, Charlotte?"

Charlotte: (Playful) "Well, there's the unspoken rule that you must master the art of sneezing silently to avoid disturbing fellow readers."

Lucas: (Grinning) "Sneezing stealth mode, got it. By the way, when I'm not perfecting my sneeze-suppression technique, I'm a fan of outdoor adventures. How about you, Charlotte? Any secret hobbies or preferred pastimes in the realm of non-library adventures?"

Note: Lucas uses the chaos of the library as his opening line, which Charlotte finds amusing. The playful banter revolves around the relatable aspects of library behavior. Lucas transitions into asking about Charlotte's hobbies and preferences, maintaining a light and playful tone.

🚌 Icebreakers for Public Transportation Settings

Don't let your journey be a silent one – whether you're on a train, bus, subway, or even a plane, I've got the perfect conversation starters to make those rides unforgettable. From station to station, these icebreakers will transform your transit time into a lively adventure. So, whether you're waiting at the platform, riding the bus, zipping through tunnels, or soaring through the skies, get ready to connect with fellow travelers and make your commute a memorable one!

For Airport:

- "Hey, do you think this place is secretly a hub for undercover superheroes?"
- "Hey there, I heard the vending machines here are basically treasure chests of snacks. Any recommendations?"
- "Hi! Ever played the 'guess the destination' game based on people's luggage?"
- "Hello! Do you think we're all secretly characters in a massive book of 'Adventures in Airports'?"
- "Hey! Do you think airports could host a reality show based on passengers' stories?"

For Airplane:

- "Hi there! Ready to conquer the in-flight entertainment together?"
- "Hey! I guess we're seat neighbors for this journey. Mind if I introduce myself?"
- "Hello! Flying is much better when shared. How's your travel day going?"
- "Hi! I have a theory that airplane conversations are like bonus travel experiences. Agree?"
- "Hi! Do you think the airplane seat is the ultimate place for

pondering life's mysteries?"

● "Hey! Can we all agree that the 'getting comfy in an airplane seat' ritual is an Olympic sport?"

For Train Station:

● "Hi! Do you think train stations have a secret recipe for creating endless delays?"

● "Curious: Do you have a favorite type of train announcement voice? I'm team 'calm and collected'."

● "Hi! Is there a strategy for picking the perfect waiting spot at train stations?"

● "Hello! I'm curious – do you have any secret talents for passing the time at train stations?"

● "Hey! Ever played the game of predicting the train's exact arrival minute?"

For Train:

● "Hey! Do you think train rides secretly turn us all into amateur detectives, trying to decode each station's secrets?"

● "Hi there! I've always wondered if train windows double as mini-movie screens. What's your favorite 'viewing'?"

● "Hey! Between us, are train stations actually ninja training grounds for mastering the art of waiting?"

● "Hi! I have a theory: trains are like mobile time machines, taking us through mini adventures. What's your take?"

● "Hey there! Are you team 'gazing out the window' or 'exploring train snacks' during the ride?"

For Bus Stop:

● "Hi! "Ever tried to guess the average miles these benches have witnessed?"

- "Hey there! Got any bus stop survival tips to share?"
- "Hi! Mind if I join you in this bus stop adventure?"
- "Hello! Do you think benches secretly have preferences for certain passengers?"
- "Hey! Any chance you've mastered the art of bus arrival prediction?"

For Bus:

- "Hey! Is it just me, or does the bus sometimes feel like a portal to a whole new adventure?"
- "Hi there! Do you think the bus seats are secretly auditioning for the comfiest throne?"
- "Hey! I've got a theory that bus rides are like mini time capsules of shared experiences. Agree?"
- "Hi! Ever imagined what the bus windows would say if they could share their views?"
- "Hey there! Can we all agree that the 'finding the best seat' quest is the real bus challenge?"

For Subway Station:

- "Hi! Any hidden subway station gems you'd recommend exploring?"
- "Hey there! Ever imagine what subway trains would say if they could talk?"
- "Hi! Is there a secret code for deciphering subway maps like a Pro?"
- "Hello! Curious if you've encountered any subway station mysteries?"
- "Hey! Do you think subway rides are like short stories with unique characters?"

For Subway Train:

- 🗨 "Hi! Is it just me, or does the rhythm of the train remind you of a giant subway symphony?"
- 🗨 "Hey there! Do you have any secret strategies for snagging the best seat on the train?"
- 🗨 "Hi! Have you ever imagined what the subway train's 'theme song' would be?"
- 🗨 "Hi! Mind if I sit here, or is this a prime 'people-watching' spot?"
- 🗨 "Hi! Do you think subway rides are like mini adventures?"

🐿 Example of an approach while waiting for the bus:

Setting: A bus stop on a sunny afternoon with a group of people waiting for their buses. Ethan approaches Alice, who is standing near the bus stop sign.

Ethan: (Grinning) "Hi! Is this the world-famous 'waiting for the bus' championship podium?"
Alice: (Chuckling) "Haha, close enough. Just missing the gold medal."
Ethan: (Playful) "Ah, I see. So, is silver a respectable achievement in this prestigious sport?"
Alice: (Smirking) "Silver is good, but we're all secretly aiming for that elusive bus stop crown."
Ethan: (Laughing) "The bus stop crown, huh? Is it bedazzled with missed buses and epic tales of waiting?"
Alice: (Amused) "Absolutely, and it comes with an exclusive 'bus delay frustration' pin."
Ethan: (Grinning) "Sign me up for that pin collection. By the way, I'm Ethan."
Alice: (Friendly) "Nice to meet you, Ethan, I'm Alice."
Ethan: (Playful) "So, any other bus stop secrets you're willing to

share, Alice?"

Alice: (Friendly) "Well, there's the unwritten rule of pretending to check the time repeatedly when you're impatient."

Ethan: (Playful) "Ah, the timeless art of time-checking. Solid strategy. How about perfecting the art of bus stop small talk?"

Alice: (Smiling) "Oh, that's a classic. You must master the weather commentary and the subtle nodding in agreement."

Ethan: (Chuckles) "Weather commentary and nodding noted. Let's say you're the reigning champion of bus stop wisdom, what's your next tip?"

Alice: (Teasing) "Oh, that's the advanced level. It involves mastering the 'bus arrival prediction dance' while looking casual."

Ethan: (Laughs) "The 'bus arrival prediction dance' – I'm intrigued. I'll definitely need lessons. By the way, Alice, aside from bus stop skills, any other talents in your repertoire?"

Alice: (Friendly) "Well, I'm a self-proclaimed trivia whiz and an amateur doodle artist."

Ethan: (Curious) "Trivia whiz and doodle artist? I might just be the luckiest person at this bus stop. Any chance I'll get a glimpse of those doodles?"

Alice: (Blushing) "Maybe if you promise not to critique them too harshly."

Note: In this playful conversation, Ethan initiates a light-hearted interaction with Alice by using a funny and relatable observation about waiting at a bus stop. Alice engages naturally, and the conversation revolves around humorous insights into bus stop experiences and shared interests. The playful banter helps establish an engaging connection between Ethan and Alice.

♟ Example of an approach on a subway train:

Setting: Inside a subway train during the evening commute. The subway car is moderately crowded with passengers, and Iris is seated near the window. Asher, standing nearby, initiates a conversation with his lighthearted question about subway seats and their comfort levels.

Asher: (Friendly) "Hey there! Quick question: Do you think subway seats are secretly in a race to see who can be the most comfortable?"

Iris: (Confused but intrigued) "Huh? Oh, um, I guess I never thought about it that way."

Asher: (Grinning) "No worries, it's a bit of a random thought. By the way, I'm Asher."

Iris: (Smiling) "Nice to meet you, Asher. I'm Iris."

Asher: (Engaging) "So, Iris, have you ever imagined subway seats having personalities? Like, they're each trying to win us over?"

Iris: (Chuckling) "Okay, that's kind of amusing. I suppose they could be like undercover comfort agents."

Asher: (Laughs) "Exactly! And you know what? I have a sneaking suspicion that the one over there is the ringleader."

Iris: (Playfully) "Oh, definitely. You can tell by its confident distinguished aura."

Asher: (Playfully) "So, are you a daily subway superstar, or more like a 'subway whenever you feel like it' kind of person?"

Iris: (Smiling) "First one I guess, gotta stick to the routine for work. How about you?"

Asher: (Grinning) "Me too. But every now and then, I can't resist the temptation to take a spontaneous detour and see where it leads. Have you ever had any subway adventures?"

Iris: (Thinking) "No, I don't recall I have. You, ever found something unexpected on your detours?"

Asher: (Playfully) "Absolutely! Earlier, I stumbled upon a girl named Iris. She is such a fun person to talk to. I wonder what she thinks about me."

Iris: (Blushing and grinning) "She thinks you might be the most surprising thing today. Are you always that chatty?"

Asher: (Grinning) "Well, Iris, I'm usually just a 'subway thoughts' kind of guy, but you've got me breaking out of my shell. It's not every day I meet someone as fun and engaging as you. Are you always that quick-witted?"

Note: In this interaction, Asher began with an offbeat and humorous question about subway seats, which was intended to break the ice and create a relaxed, enjoyable atmosphere.

As the conversation progresses, Asher smoothly transitions to personal questions about Iris's subway habits and her experiences, which helps build a connection and provides a natural flow to the conversation.

Asher continues by playfully expressing his curiosity about her opinion of him. Iris responds with a compliment and a light tease about his chattiness. He returns the compliment and shares how Iris has made the conversation enjoyable for him. This exchange reflects mutual interest and a growing connection between the two.

Icebreakers for Women Sitting on Benches in Outdoor Settings

When you spot a woman enjoying the fresh air and taking a seat on a park bench or any outdoor spot, don't miss the chance to turn that tranquil moment into a delightful conversation. Whether it's a sunny day at the park, a bustling city square, or a charming garden, I've curated the perfect icebreakers to help you strike up a chat and make the most of those outdoor vibes. So, take a seat beside her, spark a smile, and let the conversation bloom in the beauty of nature.

- "Mind if I join the 'standing tall' club?"
- "Is this bench-stilts training? Can I sign up?"
- "Impressive bench view. Mind if I grab a seat nearby?"

- "Is this the VIP section of the park?"
- "Is standing on benches the latest park workout?"
- "Did I miss the memo about bench-standing Olympics?"
- "Hey, I heard benches are the new stages for park performances. Can I watch?"
- "I've always thought benches were for sitting. Mind if I get in on the trend?"
- "You've mastered bench acrobatics. Can I have a mini-lesson?"
- "Do you have insider information on the park's official bench-standing contest?"
- "I'm starting to think park benches are underrated as stages for impromptu performances. What's your act?"
- "Mind if I join the elite 'standing on a bench' club?"
- "Excuse me, I heard this bench offers the best view in the park. Is that true?"

🗫 Example of an approach in a park:

Setting: A picturesque urban park on a sunny afternoon, with lush greenery, a serene pond nearby, and scattered park benches. Owen is about to initiate a playful conversation with Carla, who is sitting on one of the park benches, wearing earphones and looking at her phone.

Owen: (Smirking, mimicking the action of removing earphones) "Excuse me, I hope this isn't an odd question, but does this bench have a two-person limit? I've heard rumors about rebellious benches breaking rules."

Carla: (Chuckling, removing earphones) "Haha, no limits, I guess."

Owen: (Grinning) "Great to hear. Mind if I test its hospitality? I promise I won't overload its social calendar."

Carla: (Smiling) "Sure, go ahead."

Owen: (Sitting down) "Thanks. I'm Owen."

Carla: (Smiling) "I'm Carla."

Owen: (playful) "So, what's the verdict? Does this bench have the perfect view for a phone screen escape?"

Carla: (Briefly) "Definitely"

Owen: (Playful) "Ah, the ultimate entertainment choice. And here I thought the squirrels were the park's main attraction. So, do you think squirrels ever host dance parties?"

Carla: (Smiling) "Maybe."

Owen: (Smiling) "You know, I've always suspected squirrels have some hidden moves. So, any fascinating virtual adventures?"

Carla: (More Engaged) "Oh, just some YouTube videos. They make the time pass."

Owen: (Curious) "Nice! Any recommendations? I'm always up for discovering new rabbit holes of online entertainment."

Carla: (Opening Up) "Well, if you're into cute animal antics, there's this channel that compiles hilarious pet bloopers."

Owen: (Enthusiastic) "Ah, the universal language of funny pet moments. Count me in as a fellow aficionado. Beyond bench discussions, what else keeps you entertained, Carla?"

Carla: (More Talkative) "Well, I love trying out new baking recipes and occasionally challenging my friends to board game showdowns."

Owen: (Engaging) "Baking and board games, a fantastic combo. Ever created a dessert masterpiece while scheming your next Monopoly win?"

Carla: (Laughing) "Not yet, but it's a tempting idea."

Note: Owen playfully approaches Carla, using a lighthearted question about the bench's seating capacity. He successfully directs her attention away from her phone and earphones and engages her in conversation. Owen adeptly transitions from Carla's brief responses to more engaging topics, like her interests and online activities.

♫ Icebreakers That Can Be Used When a Woman Is Wearing Earphones or Using Her Phone in Various Situations

Who says smartphones and earphones are immune to the power of a well-timed icebreaker? Don't worry, I've got your back in navigating the modern maze of devices and distractions. Get ready to defy the digital odds with these clever icebreakers, designed to make her smile even when she's lost in the world of screens. It's time to show that technology and charm can coexist!

- "Hi! Are you lost in a podcast world or just exploring new sonic dimensions?"
- "Hey there! Is your phone a source of wisdom, entertainment, or a bit of both?"
- "Hi! I'm guessing that book or podcast is pretty captivating. Care to share the title?"
- "Hey! Is your phone an undercover superhero, saving us from boredom?"
- "Hi there! I'm curious, Is your playlist setting the mood for world domination or just relaxation?"
- "Hey! I can't help but wonder if your earphones are playing a theme song for your journey."
- "Hi! Is that phone your co-pilot or your ticket to an alternate reality?"
- "Hey there! I'm guessing that app has unlocked the secrets of life or just cat videos?"
- "Hey! Are you multitasking like a pro or just enjoying some quality tunes?"
- "Hi there! Your phone seems like a trove of mysteries. Any recent discoveries?"
- "Hey! Are you on a mission to find the perfect soundtrack

for this train adventure?"

- "Hi! Is that podcast episode so captivating that even the train's announcements can't interrupt?"
- "Hey there! I'm curious, Are you on a voyage through virtual reality or catching up on reality?"
- "Hi! I have a feeling your phone holds the secrets of the cosmos. Or maybe just funny memes?"
- "Hi there! I can't help but wonder what awesome playlist you're rocking right now."
- "Hey! Are you on a mission to discover the best train-ride soundtrack?"
- "Hi! I'm curious, Is that book or podcast so engaging that even the train journey can't distract you?"
- "Hey there! Is your phone secretly a portal to another dimension, or just the latest memes?"
- "Hi! I've got a challenge for you: Can you switch from 'train traveler' to 'train talker' for a quick chat?"

Note: In some cases, to prevent repeating your initial question or observation, which she might not have heard due to her earphones, you can use a non-verbal cue like mimicking the action of removing earphones, as demonstrated in the previous example. Additionally, after your phone or earphones-related icebreaker, you can smoothly transition to another contextual icebreaker. Let's illustrate this scenario:

Guy: "Hi! I've got a challenge for you: Can you switch from 'train traveler' to 'train talker' for a quick chat?"
Girl: "What do you want to chat about?"
Guy: "Well, I heard that if you chat about trains with a fellow passenger on a train, you will have the most awesome day ever. So, what do you think is the most annoying thing about trains?"
Girl: "Oh, that's a tough one. Well, I'd say it's when your fellow passengers decide to have a phone conversation with the volume

cranked up to maximum. It's like a live podcast that you never wanted to subscribe to. How about you?"

Guy: "Oh, absolutely! Those impromptu phone conferences can turn a peaceful train ride into a surprise episode of 'Loud Talkers Unleashed.' I couldn't agree more. But for me, it's the classic 'rush hour sardine can' experience. You know, when everyone's crammed in, and personal space becomes a distant memory. What's your survival strategy for crowded trains?"

Girl: "Haha, well, I've mastered the art of strategic positioning. I strategically choose a spot where I'm less likely to get squished. It's all about balance and some subtle elbow maneuvers. But seriously, it's an adventure every time. Any epic train stories to share?"

② Nightlife Settings

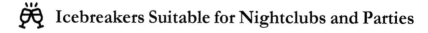 Icebreakers Suitable for Nightclubs and Parties

Stepping into the vibrant world of nightclubs and parties opens the door to endless possibilities for connection and fun. To help you make an unforgettable impression in these electrifying settings, here are some icebreakers that are perfectly tailored to the lively atmosphere. Whether you're looking to initiate conversations, break the ice, or simply have a blast, these playful approaches are your ticket to creating memorable moments on the dance floor:

- "Hi! What do you think about me so far?"
- "Hey there! Are you dancing like nobody's watching, or is this your secret talent show?"
- "Hi! If the DJ took requests, what song would you choose to set the party on fire?"
- "Hey! I've got a theory that dance floors are like time machines. What era are we grooving to?"
- "Hi there! Can we agree that party snacks have a mysterious

way of disappearing?"

- "Hey! Between glow sticks and dance moves, which one brings out your inner superstar?"

- "Hi! Is this your signature dance move or just a sneak peek into your dance vocabulary?"

- "Hey there! Midnight confessions: Have you ever claimed the title of 'dance floor champion'?"

- "Hi! Let's solve a party mystery: What's the secret ingredient in the punch that makes us dance?"

- "Hey! Is the party music setting the mood for the ultimate night of fun or just good vibes?"

- "Hi there! I've got a challenge for you: Can you spot the dance move that's taking over tonight?"

- "Hey! Are you a 'dancing until sunrise' enthusiast or a 'making every move count' artist?"

- "Hi! If dance battles were Olympic sports, do you think you'd bring home the gold?"

- "Hey there! Ever tried party physics: How to dance and hold a drink without spilling?"

- "Hi! Curious: Do you think dance moves can tell us more about a person than words?"

- "Hey! Let's decode the dance floor's energy: What's the vibe you're picking up on?"

- "Hey are You up for a Nonboring Conversation?"

- "If you had to describe your night in emojis so far, which ones would you pick?"

- "Hi! (pause) I forgot my killer icebreaker. But you know what, you look like a girl that I'd love to meet. I'm [your name]"

- "My parents told me not to talk to strangers, but I'll make an exception for you."

- "You see my friend over there? He wants to know if you think I'm cute."

🗨 Example of an approach in a nightclub:

Setting: The nightclub is alive with music thumping, colorful lights flashing, and people dancing. The energy is electric, and conversations buzz around the bar area. Amidst the lively atmosphere, Jacob catches Lily's eye from across the room. He confidently makes his way through the crowd, heading straight toward her.

Jacob: (Playful) "Hi! What do you think about me so far?"

Lily: (Grinning) "Well, you haven't spilled your drink on me, so that's a good start!"

Jacob: (Laughs) "True, I'm nailing this so far. But wait until I show you my dance moves later."

Lily: (Teasing) "I'll be the judge of that. What's your signature move?"

Jacob: (Exaggerating) "Ah, it's a closely guarded secret, but it involves some dramatic air guitar and a moonwalk."

Lily: (Laughing) "Oh, I can't wait to see that! But seriously, what brings you out tonight?"

Jacob: (Winks) "The chance to meet someone as interesting as you, obviously. Or maybe it's just the promise of a great dance-off."

Lily: (Amused) "Well, you've got some competition on the dance floor, but I'm up for the challenge."

Note: Jacob and Lily's playful banter continues after their initial eye contact, setting the tone for a fun and lighthearted conversation in the lively nightclub ambiance. Jacob's confident approach adds to the flirtatious atmosphere as they get to know each other better.

👥 Icebreakers for Group Integration: Welcoming Girls to Join Your Crew

In nightlife settings, inviting an entire group of girls to join your crew can be a fantastic move, especially when there's dancing involved. Here's how to make it happen:

- "Now you have to stop. You make all the other girls jealous. But you know what, come join us, and let's show them where the real party is."
- "Hey there, we were just discussing world domination. Care to join our plotting session?"
- "Hey there, we're the official 'Good Vibes Squad,' and we've got a spot reserved for you. Ready to join the party?"
- "I heard laughter and good vibes were missing from our group. Mind filling the vacancies?"
- "Is this where the party's at? We were just about to start a dance-off. You in?"
- "We've got an opening for 'Life of the Party' positions. Ready to audition?"
- "Alright, we have an opening for the 'Life of the Party' position in our group. Are you up for the challenge?"
- "You must be professional party crashers, but lucky for us, we're hiring."
- "Excuse me, but our fun quota just isn't being met. Care to lend your expertise?"
- "Quick poll: Who's in the mood for an upgrade to a VIP party experience?"
- "I've been granted the power to grant party wishes – yours is to join our legendary group!"

Note: Remember, the key is to keep it light, playful, and genuinely inviting. Your goal is to make them laugh and feel comfortable joining your group for a great time!

③ Methods for Both: Daytime and Nightlife Settings

■ The Old School Bumping into Her by "Mistake"

Well, this is what I consider a timeless classic in the art of approaching. But don't let the term "old school" fool you – this technique is far from outdated. Unlike some recognizable pickup strategies, this one involves a scenario that plays out naturally. After all, people bump into each other every day, and the innocent appearance of an accident is precisely what keeps this tactic evergreen. This approach is a favorite among many guys because it provides a smooth entry point for initiating a conversation with a girl. Picture this: You accidentally bump into her, and then you skillfully turn the encounter into a lighthearted opening line. It's a simple move that can kick-start a conversation in an unexpectedly delightful way.

However, while this tactic holds great potential for sparking a conversation, it's essential to be mindful of possible pitfalls. The "bump" should be gentle – just enough to catch her attention without startling or causing any harm. This applies not only to her physical well-being but also to her outfit. If you notice that she's holding something precious like a phone or a drink, it's best to err on the side of caution and refrain from attempting the bump. After all, you wouldn't want to send a USD1000 phone plummeting or accidentally spill a drink on her exquisite dress. When employing this approach, a sense of discretion and consideration goes a long way.

Now, let's dive into some playful remarks that can serve as icebreakers following a serendipitous bump:

- 🗨 "I think fate's trying to set up a hilarious meet-cute for us."
- 🗨 "Oops, my bad! I guess my dance moves need some work.

Hope I didn't mess up your groove too much."

- "Whoa, sorry! I promise I'm not auditioning for a new dance move."
- "My bad, I must be practicing my 'bump into beautiful people' routine."
- "Oops, I guess I was following my 'random collision' GPS."
- "You know, they say bumping into someone is the modern-day way of saying 'hello.'"
- "Looks like fate decided to introduce us in the most adorable way possible."
- "Clearly, my dance moves are just too irresistible for gravity to resist."
- "Whoa, watch out for that gravity, it's been conspiring against me all night."
- "Note to self: learn to navigate a room without causing love-at-first-bump."
- "I swear I'm not practicing for a bumper car championship; just couldn't resist bumping into you."

🐾 Example of an approach after a bumping:

Setting: It's a lively nightclub with pulsing music, colorful lights, and a crowded dance floor. Ivy is standing near the bar, chatting with friends when Luke accidentally bumps into her.

Luke: (playfully) "Sorry! I think fate's trying to set up a hilarious meet-cute for us."
Ivy: (laughs) "Well, fate certainly has a unique way of bringing people together. Are you always this smooth?"
Luke: (grinning) "Only when fate is involved. So, what's your superpower?"
Ivy: (teasingly) "I can predict the next song the DJ's going to play. What about you?"
Luke: (winks) "I have the incredible ability to make people

laugh, even when they've just been bumped into at a crowded nightclub."

Ivy: (laughs) "Impressive! You might be onto something there."

Note: Luke strikes up a playful conversation with Ivy after bumping into her. Their banter is infused with humor as they continue chatting, finding common interests and sharing more laughs as the night unfolds.

📲 The "Virtual Assistant" method

If you're a numbers game fan who prefers cutting to the chase and aiming for her number without engaging in a conversation, this method might be your cup of tea. But the genesis of this approach arose from those instances when time is short, or when the girl is with her group, possibly feeling uncomfortable conversing with a stranger or sharing her number in front of her friends or colleagues.

In essence, this method[2] involves presenting her with a message on your phone, giving her the discretion to respond by sharing her number. And the best part? Her companions need not be any wiser. They'll see her scribbling something on your screen, but in their eyes, you're someone she already knows. A discreet exchange ensues without a fuss.

To set the stage, begin by opening your "Note" app and crafting a humorous message like, "Hey, you caught my human in analysis paralysis. He's supposed to ask for your number, but he's having cold feet. Could you help him out?" Leave the text in edit mode. Now, approach your chosen lady – ideally someone whose gaze has met yours, and playfully remark, "My virtual assistant is acting out, showing me these oddball messages. Take a look!" Hand over your phone. After she reads, tap the screen to reveal the keyboard, signaling her to engage. She might just key in her digits, and that's that.

---

[2] The "Virtual Assistant" is an approach method I came up with on my own, and any similarities to existing methods are just a happy coincidence.

Here are a few potential messages that your "Virtual Assistant" might flash on the screen:

- 💬 "Hey, you caught my human in analysis paralysis. I told him to get your number, but he's hesitating. Can you help him out?"

- 💬 "I'm the digital voice of reason here. Your number would be a great addition to his contacts. How about it?"

- 💬 "I'm the tech-savvy sidekick here. Your number seems like a fantastic upgrade to his phone. Give it a go?"

- 💬 "Human alert! He's got a real knack for overthinking. How about helping him out with your number?"

- 💬 "Let's give him a push, shall we? Your number would make his day. Care to share it?"

- 💬 "I'm the digital assistant – and I say, adding your number is a smart choice. Can we make it happen?"

- 💬 "Okay, the human needs some encouragement. How about gifting him your number and making his day?"

- 💬 "Virtual assistant speaking: I've crunched the numbers, and adding your digits is the logical next step. Will you help him out?"

- 💬 "I'm here to simplify things. Sharing your number would be a great start. What do you think?"

- 💬 "You know, humans can be quite complicated. Your number would bring some order to his chaos. Care to contribute?"

Note: If you'd like to use this method as a conversation starter, you can jot down something like "Hey, you lazy human, get up and talk to her!" Once she reads it, be prepared with a follow-up like "I don't know what's gotten into my 'virtual assistant,' but things are getting quite amusing."

♟ The "Poison Pawn"

Introducing the "Poison Pawn," a technique designed to flip the script and give the ladies a reason to initiate conversation with you. You see, women and us guys are secretly playing the same game – wanting to chat but doing the "I-don't-know-what-to-say" dance. This is where the "Poison Pawn" comes to the rescue. Now, before I unravel this chess-inspired name, let's make it clear – no actual pawns were harmed in the making of this technique. In the chess world, the "Poison Pawn" is like dangling a donut in front of a dieter; irresistible. It's a bait that lures the opponent in, only to lead them to a checkmate disaster.

Bringing the "Poison Pawn" into the world of approaching women isn't about making them lose a chess piece – it's about making them think it's their ingenious plan to start a chat. Sneaky, right? This gives you the upper hand in sparking an interaction.

It's worth noting that I'm not the grandmaster behind this strategy; I just thought the name sounded cool.

So, if you're the type of guy who wouldn't trade his couch for a conversation, even if it rained gold, this technique is your hidden weapon. It's not about mustering the guts to walk over and start a chat; it's about conjuring the audacity to make her want to discuss the zaniest thing in your outfit. We're talking about that accessory or clothing item that screams "Hey, look at me!" – whether it's a funky design, a cheeky message, or an accessory that's practically waving its hand saying "Pick me!"

Picture it: You can rock an exceptional badge, an unconventional bracelet, an eye-catching medallion, a wristwatch that's so unique it might as well be from a parallel universe, or a tee with a one-liner so funny it could make a cat laugh. The possibilities are as endless as the dessert menu at an all-you-can-eat buffet.

Embrace the "quirky" and tell the "mundane" to take a hike. Your top-notch smartwatch? could easily fade into the background when compared to a timepiece with a design that shatters expectations. That shirt draping you like the one on a mannequin in a store window won't turn heads like a tee that states "I'm in the witness protection program."

Even if the girl doesn't approach you, and you're the one pressing the start button, rest assured, she'll spot your "unconventional masterpiece" and it will naturally become a conversation topic. So, make sure you're ready with a fascinating story related to that unique piece. And here's the kicker: other guys might swarm over, curious about your "fashion wizardry," and you might just find yourself in a chat with their gal pals. It's like hitting the conversational jackpot.

Now, if you're curious about wristwatches that are more outlandish than a UFO sighting, or wondering how to get your hands on one, tap into the digital jungle of e-commerce platforms, like Amazon. Simply type in keywords like "unusual wristwatches" or "weird wristwatches."

When it comes to printed tees, here's a sneak peek at the kind of messages that could turn heads and spark girls' interest:

- "I invented the color octarine – you're welcome, scientists!"
- "I can speak fluent llama – it's a hidden talent."
- "I once wrestled a unicorn and won. Ask me how!"
- "Professional time traveler – yesterday's future is today's past."
- "I have a black belt in origami – don't mess with me and my paper skills."
- "I break dance... only at really awkward moments."
- "I can hear colors. No, seriously, ask me about it!"
- "I'm a certified parallel universe tour guide – ask for a discounted trip."
- "I solved a Rubik's Cube using only my mind... and a screwdriver."
- "I'm training to be a professional cloud whisperer – I'm on Level 7 cumulus."

👕 "My pet rock thinks I'm hilarious – and he's a tough crowd."

👕 "I won a dance-off against a hologram. True story."

👕 "I'm on a first-name basis with the aliens – they're cool, by the way."

👕 "I have a PhD in sarcasm – it's a highly regarded degree."

👕 "I'm a certified expert in finding lost socks. Hire me!"

👕 "I promise I'll call tomorrow."

👕 "I'm not a morning person. Or an afternoon person. Can we meet after sunset?"

👕 "I'm not a morning person, or an afternoon person, or an evening person."

👕 "Don't follow me, I'm lost too."

👕 "A friend will help you move but a real friend will help you move a body."

4. Wrap It Up

Once you've had an enjoyable chat with a girl, it's time to transition the interaction to a point where you're either setting the foundation for future connections by getting her number, or you're creating the potential for a more intimate encounter.

In daytime settings, aiming for a hookup is often impractical due to the limited time available to build substantial connections. Therefore, securing her number becomes the optimal choice. However, in nightlife settings, the pursuit of a phone number might fall short. This is because the atmosphere lends itself to more immediate connections, with many girls being open to hookups rather than just exchanging numbers. In these scenarios, aiming for at least a kiss can be a more fitting goal.

Admittedly, requesting a girl's number might sometimes feel a tad unconventional, even after an engaging conversation. However, in reality, it's a natural progression. The key lies in maintaining a light, positive tone that aligns with the playful atmosphere you've established. A clever approach is to offer her a glimpse of the excitement she can anticipate if she shares her number. Consider these illustrative examples:

- "I've enjoyed talking to you. Let's make sure our paths cross again. Pop your number into my phone and we'll make some fun plans!"
- "If you're up for continuing this conversation, drop your number in my phone. It's like an exclusive VIP pass to more laughter and good vibes."
- "I have this theory that numbers can be magical, especially when they lead to awesome conversations. Slide your digits into my phone, and let's make some magic happen."
- "Your laughter deserves an encore. Share your number, and I'll make sure we keep the good times rolling with more jokes, stories and smiles."
- "Hey, you know, this conversation has been so much fun. I feel like we're just getting started. Pop your number in my phone and let's keep the momentum going!"
- "I've got a theory: great conversations should never end. What do you say we keep this one going? Slide your number into my phone, and let's make it happen!"
- "I have this feeling that our chat doesn't want to end here. How about we take it to the next level? Tap your number in my phone, and we'll make sure it doesn't."
- "You've got such a cool vibe; I'd hate for it to end right here. How about we make a pact? You tap your number in my phone, and we'll make sure this awesome convo continues."
- "I'm all about making connections with awesome people. Ready for the next step? Pop your number into my phone, and let's stay connected!"
- "I've had a blast talking with you, and I'm not ready for it to end. Ready for an encore? Tap your number in my phone, and let's keep the good times rolling."

- 🗨 "I've got a rule: if I meet someone awesome, I make sure to stay in touch. Ready to follow the rule? Tap your number in my phone and let's keep this going!"
- 🗨 "Our conversation is a story I want to keep reading. Help me turn the page – tap your number in my phone, and let's write the next chapter."

As you can tell, diving into the sea of approaching women is like embarking on a hilarious adventure ride that could potentially land you in a relationship station! But hey, before we talk about dating apps, remember to:

- ❏ **Read the Situation:** No, we're not talking about deciphering hieroglyphics here. Just tune in to her vibes and the atmosphere around. If it feels like the stars are giving you the thumbs-up and the setting is as chill as a penguin on vacation, then go ahead and make that move.
- ❏ **Confidence and Delivery:** Imagine strutting in with the suaveness of a penguin doing the moonwalk. Flash her a smile that's more contagious than a giggling dolphin, and remember, confidence is your co-pilot on this fun ride. If you deliver the line with confidence and a playful tone, it's more likely to come across as charming rather than awkward.
- ❏ **Respect Boundaries**: Now, we're all about playfulness, but remember to respect personal space like a cat guarding its nap spot. If she's giving off vibes colder than a snowman's nose, take the cue gracefully and glide on to the next adventure.
- ❏ **Embrace the Outcome:** Just like a roller coaster, not every twist and turn will have you screaming with delight. Be ready for a mix of reactions – from a grin wider than a dolphin's flipper to a raised eyebrow that could challenge an owl's wisdom. Keep that positive spirit intact no matter where this wild ride takes you.

Chapter 4
THE ONLINE ODYSSEY

Well, the time has come to delve into the realm of online dating. However, it's crucial to clarify precisely what I mean by "online dating." In this context, I've referring to dedicated dating apps like Tinder, Bumble, Hinge, or eHarmony. We're not discussing the broader social media platforms like Instagram or Facebook. While some adventurous souls do attempt to unearth romantic connections on social media, it's imperative to grasp that these platforms were not designed with dating in mind. Attempting to find a date on these sprawling platforms can be akin to searching for a proverbial needle in a haystack, a pursuit laden with uncertainty due to the myriad intentions of its users.

Social media giants such as Facebook and Instagram serve multifaceted purposes in our digital lives. They are the virtual town squares where we socialize with friends, share glimpses of our lives through photos, promote our businesses, and much more. It is in this dynamic milieu that the quest for a romantic partner can become an arduous task, often consuming time in vain and, in some unfortunate cases, leading to account suspensions due to unintended infractions of community guidelines.

On the contrary, dating apps are meticulously crafted to serve a singular purpose – facilitating connections between individuals seeking romantic partners. These platforms are precision instruments tailored for the art of matchmaking, and their efficiency in this regard is unparalleled. Within the realm of dating apps, you'll find a diverse community of individuals, each with their own unique intentions and desires, all brought together by the common thread of exploring potential romantic connections.

One of the distinct advantages of certain dating apps, such as eHarmony, is the employment of sophisticated matching algorithms. These algorithms, honed through years of data-driven refinement, are designed to align users with potential partners whose compatibility extends beyond mere superficial attraction. As a result, on platforms like eHarmony, your chances of encountering like-minded individuals actively seeking relationships are greatly enhanced.

Now, let's explore the diverse world of dating apps, each with its unique character and features:

1. Popular Dating Apps

Tinder

With its iconic swiping feature, Tinder has become synonymous with modern dating. It's known for a diverse user base, making it suitable for both casual encounters and serious relationships. Tinder primarily relies on location-based matching, encouraging serendipitous connections.

Tinder requires a mutual match before users can send messages to each other. In other words, both parties must swipe right on each other's profiles to establish a match and unlock messaging.

Bumble

Bumble empowers women to make the first move after a match, promoting a more balanced approach to dating. It's inclined toward fostering meaningful connections and relationships. Bumble employs matching algorithms to suggest potential partners.

Bumble, similar to Tinder, necessitates a mutual match to initiate conversations. However, once a match is made, women have the opportunity to send the first message within 24 hours.

Hinge

Hinge sets itself apart by connecting users through mutual friends on social media. It emphasizes the creation of more authentic and lasting connections. Hinge employs matching algorithms to recommend compatible profiles.

Hinge operates on the principle of mutual connections. Conversations can only begin after two users have mutually liked each other's profiles, creating a match.

OkCupid

OkCupid employs an extensive questionnaire to understand users' personalities and preferences. It's suitable for a wide range of dating goals, from casual to serious. OkCupid uses matching algorithms based on user responses.

OkCupid allows users to send messages to each other without requiring a mutual match. This approach fosters more open communication among its users.

Match.com

As one of the pioneers of online dating, Match.com offers a wide range of features and is suitable for those seeking serious relationships. It employs matching algorithms to connect users based on compatibility.

Match.com also permits messaging between users without the necessity of a mutual match. It offers a more flexible approach to initiating conversations.

eHarmony

eHarmony is known for its thorough personality assessment and compatibility matching system. Users are required to invest more time in completing their profiles due to the extensive questionnaire and the multitude of in-depth questions they need to respond to. This meticulous approach is aimed at ensuring that users receive highly compatible match suggestions, making it an excellent choice for those who are willing to invest time and effort in finding a serious, long-term relationship.

eHarmony follows a more structured approach. Users need to complete the extensive personality assessment, and the platform then suggests compatible matches with whom they can communicate.

Plenty of Fish (POF)

POF is a free dating platform with a large user base. It caters to various dating intentions, but its features are more limited in the free version compared to the paid version.

POF allows users to send messages without requiring a mutual match, offering a wider range of communication opportunities.

Paired

Paired is geared towards those looking for meaningful connections. It emphasizes video profiles for a more authentic introduction. Matching algorithms are used to suggest compatible users.

Paired allows users to send messages without a match, promoting open and unrestricted interaction.

Coffee Meets Bagel

Coffee Meets Bagel sends users a limited number of curated matches each day, encouraging quality over quantity in dating interactions. It's inclined towards fostering serious relationships.

On Coffee Meets Bagel, users are provided with a curated selection of matches each day, and conversations can commence once both parties express interest in creating a match.

Badoo

Badoo is a versatile platform known for its global user base. It caters to various dating intentions, but it's particularly popular in some regions for casual dating.

Badoo provides the flexibility to send messages without a mutual match, catering to a wide range of communication preferences.

Free vs. Paid Versions

In the world of dating apps, the transition from free to paid versions often unlocks a multitude of benefits. While free versions offer a taste of the app's functionality, limitations are commonplace. For instance, on some apps in the free version, you may not have the ability to see who views your profile or who your matches are. Moreover, sending messages or viewing received messages may be restricted, limiting your communication with potential connections. Upgrading to a paid subscription typically removes these barriers and provides a more seamless and enriched dating experience. It's an investment that many users find worthwhile in their pursuit of meaningful relationships.

Regional Variations and App Popularity

It's worth noting that the usage and popularity of these dating apps can vary significantly based on your geographical location and the ever-evolving landscape of digital dating. What might be a widely used app in one region may not have the same presence in another. Furthermore, the dating app landscape is dynamic, with new platforms emerging and user preferences shifting over time. So, as you embark on your journey into the world of online dating, keep in mind that the dating app scene you encounter may differ from the descriptions in this book. Staying informed about the current dating app trends and preferences in your specific area can be a valuable aspect of your quest for Miss Right.

2. Tips to Improve Your Online Dating Game

🧍 Your Profile

📷 Pictures

No matter which dating app you're diving into, there's a universal truth you can't escape – photos. Online dating is like a high-stakes beauty pageant; it's all about the visuals first and witty icebreakers and conversations second. So, brace yourself because those pictures are your opening act, and they've got to sing like a superstar. Your chances of scoring a match or getting a reply hinge on those precious pixels. But before we dive into the "photo magic," let's first unveil the grand spectacle of the top 5 "Photo NO-NOs" in the world of profile pictures.

 The 5 Photo Mistakes to Avoid

#1. No Fakes

Say goodbye to profiles featuring abstract art, serene landscapes, fancy cars, famous actors, or runway models. Your photos should shout "You!" from the digital rooftops. The days when you could sneak into the dating world without a profile picture or with shots that could pass for an art gallery catalog are as ancient as the pyramids. So, if your grand strategy involves reaching out from behind the curtain of fake accounts, using pictures that look like they belong in a stock photo library, it's time to hit the pause button on your reading adventure. This chapter isn't your enchanted forest. Every woman yearns for the comforting certainty that she's bantering with a living, breathing human, not a mysterious mirage. A profile filled with photos but missing the authentic "you" might trigger more alarm bells than a magician's long sleeves. She might just assume you're either married or have a hidden agenda.

#2. No Selfies!

In the lively realm of dating apps, selfies often don't make the cut when it comes to attracting potential matches. It's not about doubting your uniqueness; it's simply because these close-up shots, usually taken at awkward angles and with less-than-ideal lighting, may not show you in your best light. Furthermore, selfies often provide limited insight and can inadvertently convey a sense of narcissism or self-absorption. While selfies have their place for casual sharing and capturing personal moments, they may not always shine in the digital dating scene. Consequently, many users find that opting for alternative photos that offer a more diverse and visually engaging portrayal can enhance their dating app profiles and increase their chances of making a positive impact.

#3. No Sunglasses!

Shades off, my friend! It's time to talk about the "sunglasses co-nundrum" in dating profile pics. Sure, sunglasses can make you look like a Hollywood star, but guess what? Women are aware of this shady business. They'll think you're hiding something, and we're not talking about your secret stash of chocolate. Plus, they really, really want to see your eyes. When a woman spots your photo, it's like an eyeball treasure hunt – they go straight for the windows to your soul. So, let's get serious here. No sunglasses, caps, or hats that could transform you into the world's most enigmatic man. You want those thumbs-ups and matches, right? Well, let your peepers shine like the stars they are, and you'll be well on your way to a match made in sunglasses-free heaven!

#4. No Group Photos!

In your profile picture, it's just you, no extras. Don't turn it into a guessing game; she doesn't want to play "Where's Waldo" with your face. Trust me, when faced with group shots, she'll play detective and peg you as the "invisible man."

Oh, and don't even think about those pictures where you're the lone ranger surrounded by other ladies: it's like waving a neon sign that says, "I'm working overtime for attention!" So, stick to the one-man show for those perfect profile pics. It's your time to shine, without any distracting co-stars!

#5. No Cluttered or Distracting Backgrounds!

This isn't a strict "NO," but it's like cleaning your room before a date – you want to make a good impression.

Now, a cluttered background can be a brain-buster. Her mind goes into overdrive processing it all, and she might swipe left faster than a kid rejects broccoli. What makes a background cluttered, you ask? Picture this: a furniture store explosion – tables, chairs, shelves – or a city block at rush hour: crowds, cars, buildings, shops.

It's recommended that your background doesn't showcase more than two people or a structure. And that structure should be an awesome one.

And here's a pro tip: avoid blending in with your background like a chameleon at a color-matching contest. If you're blond or wear lighter clothes, go for a backdrop with a darker color; if you're a brunette or wear darker clothes, opt for something a bit lighter.

These are the five deadly sins of profile pics. Commit them, and you might as well sign up for a masterclass in swiping left. Now that we've cleared these matters, let's explore the types of photos that catch a lady's eye.

Attention-grabbing pics

Full-body Reveal or Just the Bust?

In your main profile picture, it's all about that upper body, folks. You can unleash the full-body extravaganza only if your face is shining like the sun at noon. Imagine yourself perched on a railing or confidently posing on a staircase – that's the kind of full-body prowess we're talking about. But honestly, save the full-body escapades for your secondary photos; let your upper half hog the limelight in the main event.

To Smile or Not to Smile?

The eternal dilemma of profile pictures. It's like a personal comedy show, and your face is the star. Ideally, you should flash those pearly whites, but here's the catch – it needs to be as genuine as finding extra fries at the bottom of your fast-food bag.

Now, not everyone is blessed with a movie star smile. Some folks have a "unique" dental situation or treat toothpaste like an urban legend. So, if your grin could use a makeover, it's okay to go for the "serious and mysterious" look. Just be sure not to cross over into "I'm plotting world domination" territory.

The golden rule here is to go with what suits you best: if you've got a smile that can light up a room, let it shine. If your serious face could rival James Bond, then embrace your inner secret agent.

But wait, there's more! Here are some pro tips for summoning that genuine smile:

- ☼ Think of something hilarious or heartwarming.
- ☼ Play the "peek-a-boo" game with your photographer by turning away and having them call your name. When you face them, pretend you're reuniting with a long-lost friend – an instant smile is guaranteed.
- ☼ And if all else fails, recruit a cute furry sidekick. After all, who can resist a grin when there's a fluffy accomplice involved?

Eyes on Camera or Side View?

Welcome to the world of profile picture poses, where your gaze can launch a thousand swipes. Now, here's the plot twist – whether you should channel your inner model with a sidelong glance depends on your face's charisma.

Peeking sideways can give you an air of mystery, a bit like a detective in a classic film, which, let's be honest, is like catnip for the ladies. But here's the catch – not everyone pulls off the "sly fox" look. Some guys end up looking more like confused penguins.

So, if you're not sure your side-eye game is strong, it's best to go for the "straight shooter" approach and look right at the camera. But hey, if you're convinced you've got that enigmatic charm, then unleash the side-eye. And if you can master both like a pro, throw in some photos where you're the master of both worlds – it's like a two-for-one deal in the profile pic game.

With or Without a Dog?

Remember the "poison pawn" tactic we talked about in the previous chapter? Well, here's another chess move for you. When you team up with a dog, not only will you smile naturally but you also summon an army of likes. It's like having a secret weapon in your dating arsenal.

A photo with a dog packs ten times more punch than your average solo shot. So, if you've got a furry friend, get them in the picture with you. Don't have a dog? No problem. Ask a friend or even a stranger who's walking their friendly pup if you can snap a quick pic together. People are usually happy to help, and you might make a new friend in the process.

But hold on, we're not talking about just any dog. Leave the tough guys like pit bulls and Rottweilers out of this — stick to the cute and friendly bunch.

Now, here's the secret sauce: both you and your four-legged buddy should radiate pure joy in the photo. No one wants to see a dog giving you the "save me" look or a "get me outta here" vibe. So, channel your inner dog whisperer, and remember, a happy dog equals a swipe-right magnet.

Outdoor or Indoor Pictures?

Let's dive into the world of lighting. Photos captured in natural light have a magical touch that can make anyone look their best, while indoor shots often lack that charm. So, the verdict is clear: opt for the great outdoors. When it's time to snap your profile pics, head outside during the daytime, preferably on sunny days. Your profile will thank you, and potential matches will be captivated by your radiant outdoor aura.

With or Without Eyeglasses?

Now, when it comes to glasses in your profile picture, it's not a deal-breaker either way. Whether you proudly wear your glasses or prefer the glasses-off look, it's entirely up to you. But if you're leaning towards glasses-off, here's a little photo hack: hold your glasses by one arm, positioned somewhere between your chin and chest.

This clever maneuver not only showcases your eyewear but also adds an intriguing twist to your photo.

Props or No Props?

Now, let's talk about props, the magical ingredients that can turn a regular photo into a captivating masterpiece. Props are like the secret sauce of your dating profile. Imagine you have a talent, like playing the guitar or taking mesmerizing photos; why not flaunt it? Grab that guitar or camera and let's get creative!

If you're the Spielberg of your friend group, have someone snap a pic while you're filming your cinematic masterpiece or just casually hold your camera like you own the place. If you're a musical virtuoso, strike a chord with a photo of you serenading with your instrument of choice. And if extreme sports are your jam, show off your daredevil spirit in action.

Now, here's the secret sauce: When you're showcasing your talents, you can choose to give your prop some love. If it's a guitar, gaze at it like it's the love of your life. This pic will grab her attention and spark her curiosity to explore the rest of your profile. But here's the rule: one talent show photo is enough. After all, variety is the spice of dating app life!

Phone or Camera?

We've all faced the choice: relying on your trusty smartphone or opting for the big guns, like a DSLR camera from Nikon, Canon, or Sony. It's decision time.

If you're lucky enough to have a DSLR at your disposal, don't hesitate – grab it. No need to overthink it. The fact remains: photos taken with a proper camera are in a league of their own. It's like comparing a five-star meal to a drive-thru burger. Your profile deserves that extra helping of visual appeal, right?

Original or Blurry Background?

Now, if you have a picture where you look great but the background is unsightly or cluttered, here's a nifty trick to make yourself stand out: give it the classic blur treatment. You can achieve this effect either when taking the photo using a DSLR camera or later on in a photo editing program like Photoshop (if you're skilled in that department). Some phones also offer a blur effect through their default photo viewing apps, but the results might not be top-notch.

Picture this: you, sharp as a tack, with a background that's as blurry as your memories after a wild party. It's like putting the spotlight on yourself while politely shushing the chaos behind you. Now, isn't that picture-perfect?

The Quantity and Variety of Pics

Unlike social media profiles that resemble a digital scrapbook, dating apps are more like a curated gallery. So, you don't need to flood your profile with pictures. In fact, four photos should do the trick, even though these apps often let you upload more – quality over quantity, right?

For your main photo, it's time to deploy what I fondly call the "poison pawn pic." This is your secret weapon, your chance to shine. It can be the one where you're charmingly accompanied by a dog, or maybe you're showcasing a talent that's sure to impress. Basically, it's the picture that presents you in a way that makes her stop and think, "Well, this guy's not your run-of-the-mill swiper."

Now, onto the other three photos. These should transport her to different natural settings – think picturesque landscapes from your travels. Show off your adventurous side, and let her imagine herself exploring those beautiful places with you.

Oh, and a pro tip for this gallery: change up your outfits. We don't want her to think you wear the same thing every day. After all, you're a man of style and substance, and your photos should reflect that.

Tips for Improving Your Photos if You're Not Photogenic

Let's face it; Not all of us were born with the effortless charm of a runway model. If your photos usually have friends asking, "Is that really you?" or "Did you blink when they took the picture?" – fear not, there's hope! Here are some tricks to make those photos pop, even if you're convinced your camera has a vendetta against you.

- **Fashion Faux Pas:** First off, let's talk wardrobe. Are you a sporty T-shirt kind of guy, but it seems like the camera disagrees? Don't worry, it happens to the best of us. Try out different outfits: shirts, T-shirts, shirts with blazers, blazers over T-shirts – you get the idea. Find what flatters you best and don't forget that colors and patterns are important too; some of them might not suit you. Oh, and make sure your clothes aren't tired and tattered; even a DSLR can't fix that.
- **Hair Havoc:** Now, about that hair. If it has a knack for going haywire when a camera is around, consider a makeover. Change it up, style it differently, or if it's being particularly stubborn, you might even consider parting ways. Bald is trendy, too!
- **Strike a Pose (or Many!):** The secret to a great photo isn't just one pose that fits all; it's about variety. Try different angles: standing, sitting, leaning casually on a wall – show your

versatility. Get those hands to work – hold a cup, an ice cream cone, or even a camera. Make it look like you're living your best life!

- **A Fresh Perspective:** If you find yourself pulling a cringe-worthy expression or looking uncomfortable, have someone snap a candid shot when you're not expecting it. Sometimes, these off-guard moments capture your authentic charm better than a carefully posed photo ever could.
- **Call in the Pros:** If all else fails and your wallet doesn't mind the splurge, consider hiring a professional photographer. Those folks are like the Spielberg of profile pics, except they won't make you pretend you're fighting dinosaurs. They'll work their magic, finding the angles and lighting that make you shine. Just be honest about what you need the photos for, and they'll know how to make you look like a star.
  Now, if you hire a pro, don't forget about variety. Bring a suitcase full of outfits and tell him that you want to pose in different locations or use green screen[3] technology to whisk yourself away to far-off lands.

So, there you have it – a guide to transforming from an ordinary mortal into a photogenic sensation. Remember, even the stars have their off days, but with a little effort, you can make any camera your best friend.

Username

Your username should be as unique as you are, but let's keep it fun and memorable, folks. Think "AdventureAddictJohn" or

---

[3] Green screen technology, also known as chroma keying, is a technique used in photography and filmmaking. It involves shooting a subject against a bright green or blue background and later replacing that background with a different image or video during editing. In the context of profile pictures, green screen technology can be employed to transport the subject to different backgrounds, adding variety and creativity to their photos.

"GuitarGrooverGreg" – not "RandomNumberGenerator123456." Numbers are for keeping your secrets safe, not for introducing yourself in the dating app universe!

ⓘ Personal Data

This section is all about your date of birth, education, and occupation. Honesty is the name of the game, so go ahead and enter your real age. When it comes to education and work, feel free to leave those fields blank if you'd prefer not to disclose them. But please, let's skip the silly stuff like claiming you attended the "School of Life" or work at the "Happiness Factory." We're all for creativity, but let's keep it real, shall we?

📄 Profile Bio

Your bio, also known as the "About Me" section, is often the first stop for a woman once she's seen your photos. Some guys underestimate the importance of this field, assuming no one pays it any mind. But let me tell you, men may not be reading this, but women sure are.

Here's your chance to let your playful side shine with a dash of humor and flirtation. So, don't waste this precious space on dull self-descriptions or long lists of what you're looking for in a partner. Your bio's mission is to make her swipe right by sparking her interest and leaving her with the impression that connecting with you will be enjoyable and exciting. So, let's dive into some witty and playful profile descriptions to help you stand out in the dating app crowd:

Playful Call-to-Action Taglines

🔊 "Swipe right on this profile for exclusive access to witty conversations and spontaneous fun! 🚀 😄"

◄)) "Swipe right to unlock a whole new level of intriguing chats and memorable moments! 🔒😃"

◄)) "Secure your spot in a nonboring conversation by swiping right on this profile. 📱💬"

◄)) "Want to keep the good vibes flowing? Swipe right here for laughs and awesome connections! 🎉😁"

◄)) "Swipe right and unveil a world of entertaining chats and exciting rendezvous! 📱💬"

◄)) "Secure your seat on the express train to great conversations. Swipe right for a VIP pass! 🎟️🎫"

◄)) "Swipe right for a daily dose of smiles and engaging discussions. Don't miss out! 🌼💬"

◄)) "Challenge of the day: Can you swipe right faster than a text message? Show your skills and dive into vibrant chats! 📱👉"

◄)) "Tinder's prediction: Your swipe right here equals an endless stream of enjoyable interactions and spontaneous meetups! 🎉☁️"

◄)) "Tinder's friendly nudge: Swipe right on this profile to start the digital party and real-life adventures. The future looks exciting! 🎊✨"

◄)) "Swipe right if you believe in laughter, laughter, and the inexplicable allure of rubber chicken collections. 🌙😄🐔"

◄)) "Can you keep up with my pun game? Swipe right if you're up for the challenge! 😏✨"

◄)) "Swipe right for witty banter, spontaneous adventures, and a dash of sarcasm. 🐱✨"

◄)) "Swipe right if you're ready to embark on a journey of laughter and inside jokes. 😄🚀"

Note: These taglines aim to engage potential matches with humor, intrigue, and the promise of fun interactions.

Zodiac Sign-Based Descriptions

♈ **Aries:** "Aries here, always up for an adventure and a good laugh. Swipe right if you're ready to join my rollercoaster ride through life! 🎢 ♈ "

♉ **Taurus:** "Taurus who loves food, naps, and Netflix binges. Looking for someone to help me decide between pizza or tacos for dinner. 🍕 🌮 ♉ "

♊ **Gemini:** "Two-faced? Nah, just a Gemini! Swipe right if you can keep up with my endless energy and ever-changing interests. 😜 ♊ "

♋ **Cancer:** "Cancerian with a soft shell and a love for cuddles. Warning: I might steal your blanket in the middle of the night. 🦀 ♋ "

♌ **Leo:** "Leo king looking for someone to appreciate my dramatic flair and lion-like confidence. Let's conquer the world together! 🦁 ♌ "

♍ **Virgo:** "Virgo perfectionist who'll never leave home without checking the stove 10 times. Swipe right if you're ready for my organized chaos. 📝 ♍ "

♎ **Libra:** "Libra searching for balance in life and someone to help me decide on everything. Should we Netflix or go dancing tonight? ⚖️ ♎ "

♏ **Scorpio:** "Scorpio here, ready to dive deep into meaningful conversations and uncover your secrets. Don't worry; I won't sting (much). 🦂 ♏ "

♐ **Sagittarius:** "Sagittarius on a quest for adventure, exploring new places, and trying exotic foods. Let's be wanderlust partners! ✈️ ♐ "

♑ **Capricorn:** "Capricorn with ambitions higher than my favorite mountain peaks. If you're goal-oriented and love cheesy puns, swipe right! ⛰️ ♑ "

≈ **Aquarius:** "Aquarius inventor always coming up with quirky ideas and witty one-liners. Let's create a world of our own weirdness! 💡 ♒ "

♓ **Pisces:** "Pisces daydreamer seeking a partner to share deep conversations, starry nights, and spontaneous beach trips. Dive into my world! 🌑 ♓ "

Note: Feel free to mix and match these with your zodiac sign or use them as inspiration for your bio description!

Hobby-Infused Profile Descriptions

⚽ "Chess aficionado seeking a worthy opponent for epic battles of wits. Warning: I might challenge you to a real-life chess match in the park. ♟️ 👾 "

⚽ "Cycling enthusiast with a need for speed. Let's race to the nearest coffee shop – loser buys the lattes! 🚴 ☕ "

⚽ "Running through life one mile at a time. Join me for a jog and let's see if we can keep pace with each other. 🏃 🏃 "

⚽ "Fitness freak who believes in burpees and brunch. Swipe right if you're up for a HIIT workout followed by mimosas. 💪 🍸 "

⚽ "Bookworm seeking a partner in crime to explore fictional worlds together. Let's dive into some captivating novels and compare notes. 📚 ✴️ "

⚽ "Gaming nerd on a quest for a co-op partner. Prepare for epic quests, epic loot, and epic laughs. 🎮 😃 "

⚽ "Swimming enthusiast looking for a fellow mermaid. Let's make a splash and dive into some aquatic adventures. 🏊 🐠 "

⚽ "I'm a water sign, which means I'm always up for spontaneous beach trips and seaside strolls. Care to join me on a coastal adventure? 🌊 🏖️ "

⚽ "Board game aficionado seeking someone to conquer Catan

or Monopoly – but fair warning, I'm a ruthless strategist! 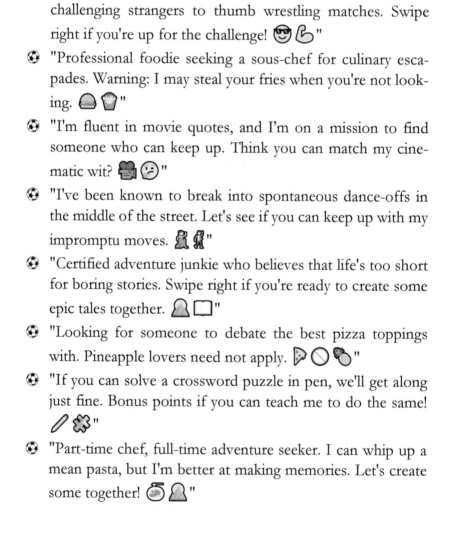"

☻ "Aspiring chef with a knack for whipping up delicious dishes. If you appreciate good food and good company, we'll get along just fine. 🍴😊"

☻ "Surfing addict who's always chasing the perfect wave. Let's ride the waves of life together and catch some epic sunsets. 🏄🏠"

☻ "Hobbies include solving Rubik's cubes blindfolded and challenging strangers to thumb wrestling matches. Swipe right if you're up for the challenge! 😎💪"

☻ "Professional foodie seeking a sous-chef for culinary escapades. Warning: I may steal your fries when you're not looking. 🍔🍟"

☻ "I'm fluent in movie quotes, and I'm on a mission to find someone who can keep up. Think you can match my cinematic wit? 🎥😉"

☻ "I've been known to break into spontaneous dance-offs in the middle of the street. Let's see if you can keep up with my impromptu moves. 💃🕺"

☻ "Certified adventure junkie who believes that life's too short for boring stories. Swipe right if you're ready to create some epic tales together. 🏔📖"

☻ "Looking for someone to debate the best pizza toppings with. Pineapple lovers need not apply. 🍕🚫🍍"

☻ "If you can solve a crossword puzzle in pen, we'll get along just fine. Bonus points if you can teach me to do the same! ✏️🧩"

☻ "Part-time chef, full-time adventure seeker. I can whip up a mean pasta, but I'm better at making memories. Let's create some together! 🍳🏠"

⚽ "Equal parts bookworm and gym enthusiast. I can discuss classic literature and squat my body weight. Let's balance intellectual debates with some fitness fun! 📚👐"

⚽ "I've got a knack for DIY projects and a soft spot for furry friends. If you're looking for someone to build a life with, I'm your handyman with a big heart. 💼🤍"

⚽ "Master of movie trivia, lover of long hikes, and always up for a spontaneous road trip. Let's write our own adventure story together! 🎥🏠🚗"

General Playful Descriptions

☺ "I excel at parallel parking and dad jokes – a rare combination. Let's see if you can guess my favorite dad joke! 🚗😄"

☺ "Part-time superhero, full-time coffee enthusiast. Looking for a partner in crime to join me on daring caffeine-fueled adventures. ☕💥"

☺ "Believer in conspiracy theories about cats secretly running the world. If you're a dog person, we can still be friends – as long as you keep an open mind. 🐱⚫"

☺ "I've got a heart of gold, a laugh that's contagious, and I'll always hold the door for you. Let's make life an adventure together! 🤍💿📱"

☺ "I might not have a superhero cape, but I'll be your everyday hero. I've got a knack for fixing things and making you smile. Ready for some fun and repairs? 🔧😄"

☺ "A mix of James Bond sophistication and goofball humor. I clean up well for fancy nights out but also love a Netflix binge in my PJs. What's your idea of a perfect date? 🕴️🍦"

☺ "I'm the guy who'll remember your favorite coffee order and never forget your birthday. I've got a sweet tooth for life, and I'm ready to share the sweetness with you! ☕🍰"

☺ "I've got a playlist for every mood and a taste for exotic cuisine. Ready to explore the world of music and food with me? 🎶☁️"

☺ "I may not have a green thumb, but I'm great at nurturing relationships. Let's plant the seeds of friendship and watch them bloom into something beautiful. 🌱🌼"

☺ "I'm a tall guy, which means I can give you the ultimate concert view – perched on my shoulders! I've got a Ph.D. in whipping up scrambled eggs and fries, so your taste buds are in for a treat. But, when it comes to flirting, I'm about as smooth as a cat on roller skates. How about you try to pick me up instead? 🔑🔍🐱"

☺ "Looking for someone to decode emojis with. Let's create our secret language! 🧸😕"

☺ "Want to be part of my epic quest for the best tacos in town? 🌮📖"

☺ "Join me in my quest for the perfect cup of coffee and exciting chats! ☕🌼💬"

☺ "Searching for a partner in crime to explore new places and share goofy moments. 🌐😋"

☺ "Looking for someone to challenge me to a dance-off! Let's groove together! 💃🕺"

Note: The key to a successful dating app bio is to be authentic and playful while giving potential matches a glimpse of your personality or interests. Feel free to use these descriptions as inspiration or modify them to align with your interests and hobbies. Adding emoticons can add a fun and visual element to your dating app bio, making it even more engaging. Feel free to use these or create your own combinations to express your personality and interests. 😊👍

The Questionnaire

If you stumble upon an app that throws a questionnaire or personality test your way, don't rush through it like you're running from a swarm of bees. Take a moment to answer those questions with sincerity. The app uses your responses to play matchmaker and dish out compatibility scores. So, let's make sure it doesn't think you're compatible with a talking potted plant, shall we?

The Swipe

If you're navigating an app with a sweeping system, like Tinder, hold your horses before you go on a wild swiping spree. It's not a numbers game, folks! Take a peek at her pictures, peruse her description, and if you're genuinely smitten, then go ahead and swipe right. But wait, why should you avoid treating that "swipe right" button like it's on fire? Let me break it down:

- **Limited Swipes Right:** Some apps offer only a limited number of right swipes in their free plan. So, here's the scoop: If you recklessly use up all your right swipes by swiping right on every profile like you're shuffling a deck of cards, you might just deplete your quota. And that means you won't even get to see a potentially perfect profile because your swipe privileges have vanished into thin air.

- **The Sketchy Bunch:** Let's establish a rule: if a profile doesn't have personal photos, proceed with caution. You never know what's lurking behind that veil of mystery. I'm not talking about physical imperfections; I'm talking about individuals using fake profiles to have a laugh at the expense of unsuspecting folks. You might even come across guys masquerading as women, so profiles without personal pictures should set off alarm bells.

⚠ **Glossy Models vs. Girl-next-door:** Keep in mind that genuine women on dating apps tend to resemble the friendly girl next door rather than professional models or Hollywood celebrities. If someone looks too good to be true, well, you know the drill – proceed with a pinch of skepticism.

⚠ **Followers' Fanatics:** If you spot her social media ID in the profile description, take a detour and swipe left. These folks are only interested in beefing up their social media following.

⚠ **Frustrated Venters:** Some women may have had their fair share of dating app mishaps, and they decide to let it all out with a lengthy profile description, ranting about the things that get on their nerves or even listing bizarre conditions like "If you're a blonde, don't even bother." Here's a tip: steer clear of these profiles, even if you happen to meet all their requirements. It's not about having preferences; it's about how they express them. Always give their profile description a read; the words might unveil a not-so-charming personality.

Now, not all women on dating apps will have multiple pictures and a profile description, so don't dismiss such profiles entirely. Just keep in mind that not everyone you encounter is a saint, and not every match will lead to a romantic rendezvous. Happy swiping!

🗩 The Icebreaker

Starting a conversation with just a "Hi" or "Hey" is like playing a silent movie in a world full of action-packed blockbusters. To stand out, you need an opening line that grabs attention. This is your moment to be the star of the show, not the supporting actor.

Craft a message that's tailored to her profile. If you spot something interesting or amusing in her photos or description, use it to your advantage. For instance, I once matched with a girl who mentioned she wanted someone to make her delete the app. My response? "So, you're looking for someone who bores you so much that you want to delete the app. I think I can help you."

So, by playfully misinterpreting her description, I sparked a delightful and engaging conversation.

However, if her profile leaves you drawing a blank, don't fret. You can always rely on a trusty general icebreaker. Here are a few examples to get the conversation rolling:

Icebreakers Based on Her Pics or Bio Description

- "I have a theory: Your profile is proof that unicorns exist 🦄✨. Am I right, or am I right?"
- "Your selfie game is strong. Are you secretly a professional Instagram influencer, or do you just know all the right angles? 📷😎😕"
- "Your photos are like a slideshow of awesomeness! 😄📷 If life were a movie, what genre would yours be: Rom-Com, Action, or Sci-Fi? 🎬💥🚀"
- "I've got to know, what's the story behind that epic hiking pic? ⛰️🥾"
- "Is that a surfboard I see in your photos? 🏄‍♀️🌊 Are you secretly a beach bum?"
- "Your smile could light up a room! 😁💡 But can it handle cheesy jokes?"
- "So, you're a foodie AND an adventurer? 🍔🌋 What's the most adventurous dish you've ever tried?"
- "I'm convinced you're a superhero in disguise. 😎🦸 What's your superpower – incredible taste in movies or the ability to make anyone smile?"
- "I see you love traveling! ✈️🌐 Any secret travel tips or

must-visit destinations?"

💬 "Your style game is on point! 👗 👓 Are you a fashion guru or just naturally chic?"

💬 "I noticed your love for books 📚 📖 – got any recommendations for a fellow bookworm?"

💬 "Your profile is a masterpiece! 🎨 🖼 Do you dabble in art or just have a knack for picking cool stuff?"

💬 "Your taste in music is as impressive as your smile! 🎶 Any chance I can be your concert buddy?"

💬 "Your yoga pose is incredible! 🧘 Care to teach me some yoga moves in person?"

💬 "You're clearly the life of the party! 🎉 When are you taking me on a night out?"

💬 "I see you're into fitness – do you have any workout tips that could make our hearts race? 💚 👍 "

💬 "Your travel photos are breathtaking! ✈️ Can I join you on your next adventure?"

💬 "With your music taste, we'd make the perfect duet! 🎤 Got any hidden talents?"

💬 "I'm intrigued by your passion for yoga and fitness. 👍 🧘 What's your secret to staying in shape?"

💬 "Exploring new places with you sounds like a dream! 🌐 Where should we jet off to first?"

💬 "Your energy for nightlife is electrifying! ⚡ Ready to dance the night away together?"

💬 "I'm all about cardio, but your smile just took my breath away! 😄 💚 When can we hit the gym together?"

💬 "I have a theory that conversations with people who have the best taste in ice cream are the most interesting. 🍦 😄 Care to prove my hypothesis?"

If she had pets in her pics:

- 💬 "Your photos with those adorable dogs really tug at my heartstrings. Are you trying to steal my heart one pup at a time? 🐶 💚 "
- 💬 "Cats in your pictures? You've officially upped your cool factor! 🐱 Are you a secret cat whisperer?"
- 💬 "Your pet photos are cute, but I'm wondering, are you as adventurous as your furry friends? 🎇 🐕 "
- 💬 "Your pics are like a zoo tour. Which animal encounter was your favorite, and can I be your next adventure? 🐹 🌴 "
- 💬 "You and your pets look like the perfect team. Are they your partners in crime for spontaneous adventures? 🐾 🐕 "
- 💬 "I see you're a fan of both cats and dogs. Are you secretly running a pet sanctuary? 🏠 🐱 🐕 "
- 💬 "With all these pet pics, I'm curious – who's the boss at home? You or the adorable animals? 🐾 👑 "
- 💬 "Your pet pics are adorable, but I bet you're the cutest one in the bunch. Want to prove me right? 😊 📷 "
- 💬 "Swiped for the dog, stayed for the human. 🐶 💚 "
- 💬 "Do you ever wonder if our pets have secret lives and throw wild parties when we're not home? My cat has that look in his eyes sometimes. 🐱 🎉 "

Note: Feel free to adapt them to better match what you've observed in her photos or learned from her description.

Icebreakers Perfect for Starting a Chat with Your Matches

- 💬 "We matched, so I guess it's official now. When's our first date? 😁 "

💬 "Congratulations, you've just matched with your future partner in crime. Ready to start an adventure? 🚀"

💬 "So, we matched. Does this mean I'm officially your new partner in fun? 🎉"

💬 "Looks like we both have great taste in swiping. How about we grab a coffee to celebrate? ☕"

💬 "Well, look at us, we matched! What's our first mission, Agent? 🕵️"

💬 "Two swipes, one match, and endless possibilities. What's our next move? 🚀"

💬 "Congratulations on your excellent choice – you matched with me! When's our victory dance? 💃"

💬 "They say matching is the first step to a great story. What's our story going to be? 📖"

💬 "We matched, so now the fun begins. What's our game plan, Captain? ⚓"

💬 "We matched! Let the epic adventures and witty conversations commence! 😄 🚀"

💬 "Well, look who we have here, a match made in digital heaven! What's our first order of business? 😄"

💬 "Our matching algorithms seem to think we'd get along. Are they onto something, or should we give them a run for their money? 😊"

💬 "Two swipes right and a match to show for it. Should we start planning our epic first date, or do you have a better idea? 🎉"

💬 "They say matches are made in heaven, but ours was clearly made on this app. What's our next step, matchmaker? 😊"

💬 "So, we both swiped right. Does this mean I can officially call you my partner in crime on this dating app adventure? 😁"

💬 "The stars aligned, and we matched! What's the cosmic plan for us, or should we write our own story? ✨"

- 💬 "I have a feeling this match could be the start of something epic. What's our first move, the dynamic duo of online dating? ✪"
- 💬 "We're officially a dating app dream team! Should we celebrate with a virtual high-five or dive right into getting to know each other? 🙌"
- 💬 "They say teamwork makes the dream work, and we've just become a team. What's our dream, and how can we make it work? ❄"
- 💬 "Two swipes and a match – it's like we won the dating app lottery! What's the jackpot prize for us, and when do we claim it? 💰"

General Icebreakers

- 💬 "Knock-Knock! 🚪 😄"
- 💬 "Pizza 🍕 or sushi 🍣 for the rest of your life? Tough choice, I know! 😄"
- 💬 "I have a confession: I'm addicted to terrible puns. Brace yourself, you might be in for a pun-tastic time! 🙈 🤪"
- 💬 "Let's settle this debate once and for all: Is pineapple on pizza a culinary masterpiece 🍍 or a culinary disaster 🍕? 😕"
- 💬 "If we could only communicate in GIFs for the next hour, which one would you send first? 😄 📷"
- 💬 "I've heard legends of mythical creatures, but I've yet to meet someone who's truly skilled at building the perfect blanket fort. Are you up for the challenge? 🏰 🛏"
- 💬 "Quick, you have to describe your perfect day in just three emojis. Go! 🌼 🍕 🎬"
- 💬 "Let's settle this age-old debate: Is a hot dog a sandwich?

The fate of foodies everywhere rests on your answer! 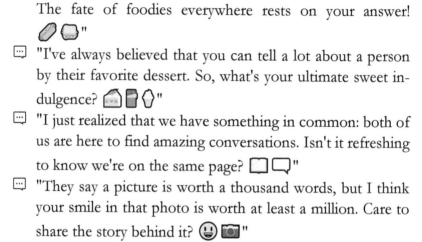"

[...] "I've always believed that you can tell a lot about a person by their favorite dessert. So, what's your ultimate sweet indulgence? 🏠🍫◇"

[...] "I just realized that we have something in common: both of us are here to find amazing conversations. Isn't it refreshing to know we're on the same page? ▢ ◻"

[...] "They say a picture is worth a thousand words, but I think your smile in that photo is worth at least a million. Care to share the story behind it? 😃 📷 "

[...] "Let's play a game of 'Two Truths and a Lie.' I'll start: I once danced in the rain 🌂, met a celebrity 🎆, and can make the world's best pancakes 🥞. What's your trio? 😕 "

Note: These icebreakers are fun and flirty, perfect for sparking conversations with potential matches if the dating app used allows chats without a match. You can also use these if her profile doesn't have anything to comment on.

🗨 The Conversation

Starting a chat on a dating app can be a bit like striking up a fun conversation at a social gathering – you want to grab her attention and make her smile. Here are some tips to keep the conversation rolling smoothly:

☀ **Short and Sweet Replies:** Think of your messages as quick, engaging remarks rather than lengthy speeches. Keep them concise, with one, two or at most three sentences per response. Sometimes there can be four if there are very short sentences. The goal is to create an enjoyable exchange, not to write a novel.

- ☼ **Sprinkle Some Emoticons:** Emoticons are like the seasoning of your messages – they add flavor and make things more interesting. But, like any good seasoning, use them in moderation. A well-placed smiley or wink can add a playful touch.

- ☼ **Playful and Light:** Save the meaningful discussions for your in-person dates. On dating apps, keep the atmosphere light, playful, and flirtatious. Discuss your jobs, hobbies, and interests, but steer clear of deep conversations.

- ☼ **No Inappropriateness:** Don't be that guy who ruins the fun with inappropriate messages or unsolicited photos. Sending explicit content is a surefire way to get blocked or, even worse, become the laughing stock of her group chat. Keep it classy, my friend. Remember, once something's on the internet, it's nearly impossible to erase. So, avoid sending anything indecent, even if she requests it – she might just be looking for some laughs with her friends.

- ☼ **The Sooner, the Better:** Don't wait too long to suggest meeting up in person. Express your interest in a face-to-face meeting early in the conversation. Confidence is attractive and shows you're serious about taking things to the next level.

- ☼ **Secure Her Number or Social Media ID:** It's perfectly understandable if she doesn't want to meet in person right away. However, it's a good idea to transition the conversation from the dating app to a more familiar chat platform like WhatsApp or social media. You can casually mention that you prefer chatting on these platforms, making it more about convenience. This step is important because profiles can be deleted, and you wouldn't want to lose contact with a potential match. Just avoid explicitly mentioning this concern; instead, emphasize the benefits of a smoother chat experience.

Here are some additional tips to make you stand out on dating app conversations:

☼ Embrace your quirks and let your unique personality shine. After all, normal is overrated!

☼ Ditch the dating clichés and whip up messages that are as original as your grandma's secret cookie recipe.

☼ Sprinkle positivity and good vibes generously, like confetti at a celebration.

☼ Steer clear of offensive or eyebrow-raising remarks, even if she throws you a curveball.

☼ Don't stick to the same old regular compliments like "You're beautiful" or "You're gorgeous." Get creative with your flattery, but be careful not to go overboard and leave them feeling overly flattered. And don't use them too frequently!

☼ Throw in some playful banter, and tease like you're auditioning for a comedy roast.

☼ Mirror her response time like a dating app chameleon. If she replies quickly, keep up the pace; if she's responding as leisurely as a sloth on a coffee break, match that rhythm.

☼ Ask questions that unravel the delicious layers of your match's personality.

☼ Don't be shy about taking a leap. After all, fortune favors the flirty!

☼ End the chat on a positive note, leaving her with a smile.

By following these tips, you can have a playful and flirty conversation that will help you connect with someone special. Now, let's explore some examples of what a playful conversation on a dating app can look like:

Example #1

Setting: Greg couldn't help but notice Lucy's captivating smile and her love for adventure in her profile pictures.

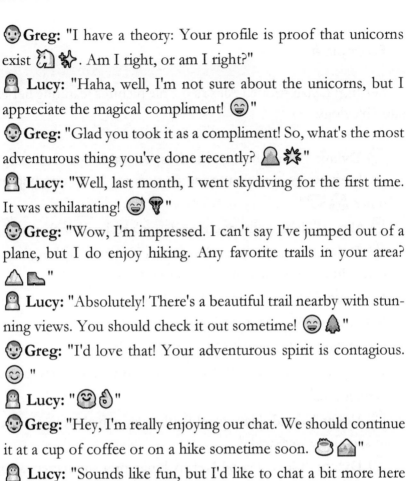

Greg: "I have a theory: Your profile is proof that unicorns exist 🦄✨. Am I right, or am I right?"

Lucy: "Haha, well, I'm not sure about the unicorns, but I appreciate the magical compliment! 😄"

Greg: "Glad you took it as a compliment! So, what's the most adventurous thing you've done recently? 🧍✨"

Lucy: "Well, last month, I went skydiving for the first time. It was exhilarating! 😄🪂"

Greg: "Wow, I'm impressed. I can't say I've jumped out of a plane, but I do enjoy hiking. Any favorite trails in your area? ⛰️🥾"

Lucy: "Absolutely! There's a beautiful trail nearby with stunning views. You should check it out sometime! 😄🌲"

Greg: "I'd love that! Your adventurous spirit is contagious. 😊"

Lucy: "😊👋"

Greg: "Hey, I'm really enjoying our chat. We should continue it at a cup of coffee or on a hike sometime soon. ☕⛰️"

Lucy: "Sounds like fun, but I'd like to chat a bit more here before meeting up. Safety first! 😊"

Greg: "Of course, Lucy, no rush at all! By the way, do you mind if we connect on Facebook? It might make chatting easier. 💗📱"

Lucy: "Sure, Greg, you can find me as [Facebook ID]. 😊"

Note: The conversation starts with Greg's playful theory about Lucy's profile. Lucy responds positively, and they chat about their adventures and hiking. Greg takes the initiative and asks Lucy out, but she prefers to chat more before meeting. He respects her decision and secures her Facebook ID to continue the conversation.

Example #2

Setting: Dylan spotted Alexa's profile pictures featuring her two adorable dogs.

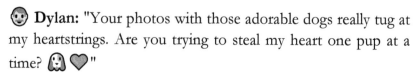

👨 **Dylan:** "Your photos with those adorable dogs really tug at my heartstrings. Are you trying to steal my heart one pup at a time? 🐶 🤍 "

👧 **Alexa:** "Haha, guilty as charged! Can't resist their charm. 😄 "

👨 **Dylan:** "I totally get it! Dogs have a way of melting hearts. Have they ever pulled any hilarious stunts at home?"

👧 **Alexa:** "Oh, you won't believe the mess they made last week! 😄 Got any funny pet stories?"

👨 **Dylan:** "Absolutely! Once, my friend's dog swiped a pizza slice right off my plate. 🍕 🐾 We should definitely swap more pet tales. 😄 "

👧 **Alexa:** "Sounds like a plan! By the way, what's your ideal way to spend the weekend?"

👨 **Dylan:** "I love a good Netflix binge or a spontaneous road trip. How about you?"

👧 **Alexa:** "Count me in for a Netflix marathon! 🎥 😊 Do you have any favorite series?"

👨 **Dylan:** "I'm all about crime documentaries lately. 😄 What about you?"

👧 **Alexa:** "I enjoy a mix of genres, but rom-coms are my favorites. 🤍 Any recommendations?"

👨 **Dylan:** "Well, if you're into rom-coms, I'd suggest trying 'Interstellar'! 🚀 "

👧 **Alexa:** "Haha, Dylan, you're taking me from romance to outer space! 😄 Maybe I'll give it a try... just for you!" 😄

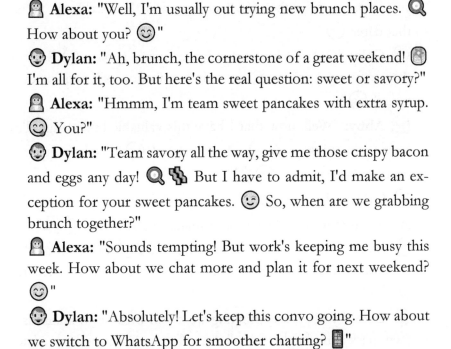

Dylan: "Exploring new frontiers, that's what I'm all about! 😄 So, aside from Netflix, what's your favorite way to spend a weekend?"

Alexa: "Well, I'm usually out trying new brunch places. 🔍 How about you? 😊 "

Dylan: "Ah, brunch, the cornerstone of a great weekend! 🍽 I'm all for it, too. But here's the real question: sweet or savory?"

Alexa: "Hmmm, I'm team sweet pancakes with extra syrup. 😊 You?"

Dylan: "Team savory all the way, give me those crispy bacon and eggs any day! 🔍 🥓 But I have to admit, I'd make an exception for your sweet pancakes. 😊 So, when are we grabbing brunch together?"

Alexa: "Sounds tempting! But work's keeping me busy this week. How about we chat more and plan it for next weekend? 😊 "

Dylan: "Absolutely! Let's keep this convo going. How about we switch to WhatsApp for smoother chatting? 📱 "

Alexa: "Sounds good! Here's my number: [WhatsApp number]. 😄 "

Note: The conversation flows from their shared love for dogs to discussing hobbies and interests, sprinkled with playful banter. Dylan successfully suggests moving the conversation to WhatsApp to continue building a connection with Alexa.

Example #3

Setting: Abby and Cole have just matched on a dating app, and they start a playful conversation.

😃 **Cole:** "We matched, so I guess it's official now. When's our first date? 😄"

👻 **Abby:** "Haha, you don't waste any time, Cole! 😄 How about you impress me with a fun fact first, and then we'll talk about that date? 😊"

😃 **Cole:** "Did you know that honey never spoils? 🍯 So, our date may be years away, but our connection will remain ever sweet! 😄"

👩 **Abby:** "Well, now that I have this valuable knowledge, I'm starting to think you're the keeper here! 😄 Got any quirkier trivia up your sleeve? 😊 📚"

😃 **Cole:** "Absolutely! Did you know that honey never spoils? I guess that makes us the sweetest match on this app. 🍯 🙏"

👻 **Abby:** "Haha, you've got me there! 🦋 🍯 So, with all this sweetness in the air, what's your idea of the perfect first date? 😄 🤍"

😃 **Cole:** "Well, I was thinking we could break into an amusement park at midnight, ride all the roller coasters, and have a late-night ice cream showdown. 🎢 🍦 What do you say, Abby? 😄 😎"

👻 **Abby:** "Haha, you're full of adventurous ideas, Cole! 🛹 I'm up for the challenge. Just make sure you bring your A-game to that ice cream showdown! 🍦 🍨"

😃 **Cole:** "You bet! I've got my ice cream tasting spoon ready! 🍦 🍴 How about we celebrate our ice cream showdown with a drink tomorrow evening? 🥤"

👻 **Abby:** "Sure, why not! Looking forward to this epic ice cream showdown and drinks tomorrow. 🍦 🥤 😄"

Note: Cole initiates contact with a flirty icebreaker, jokingly suggesting that their match means they're officially dating. Abby responds with equally playful banter about honey never spoiling, and Cole suggests a unique and fun first date idea, an ice cream showdown followed by drinks. Abby enthusiastically agrees, setting the stage for a promising and amusing first encounter.

Example #4

Setting: Jason is browsing through profiles on a dating app. He comes across Naomi's profile and is immediately drawn to her photo. He decides to send her a message, even though they are not yet a match.

😃 **Jason:** "Knock-Knock! 🚪😄"

👩 **Naomi:** "There is nobody home 🙂"

😃 **Jason:** "Oh no, I must be at the wrong door! I was hoping to meet the person who stole all the charm on this app. Guess I got lucky and found you instead. 😄"

👩 **Naomi:** "Really? 🙈🙊"

😃 **Jason:** "Absolutely! 😄 So, besides being the master of clever comebacks, do you have any other hidden talents or fun facts about yourself, Naomi? 🎉😕"

👩 **Naomi:** "I'm a passionate shopper, always on the hunt for the best deals! What about you, Jason? Tell me something intriguing! 🙂🛍️"

😃 **Jason:** "I have this knack for finding the best hole-in-the-wall restaurants wherever I go. Foodie by heart! 😄🍽️ How does a dinner date at a charming local spot sound to you? 🍽️🎆"

👩 **Naomi:** "A dinner date sounds perfect. I'll even let you pick the restaurant since you're the expert. 🍞🥟"

🙂 **Jason:** "Awesome! Let's take this to WhatsApp so we can plan our dinner date properly. What's your number?"

👤 **Naomi:** "Sure thing, Jason! It's --****."

🙂 **Jason:** "Perfect, Naomi! I've got your number, and I'll message you soon. Can't wait for our dinner date! 😄 📱"

Note: Jason kicks off the conversation with a simple and playful "Knock-Knock!" However, Naomi decides to play the classic hard-to-get game, challenging Jason's approach. Jason is aware that this is a common dynamic, so he responds with witty and flirtatious banter, complimenting and playful teasing Naomi in a bid to win her attention. The conversation eventually concludes with Jason confidently asking Naomi on a dinner date signaling his intention to continue the connection beyond the dating app. Naomi accepted his invitation and he secured her WhatsApp number, expressing his excitement for their upcoming dinner date.

After setting up a date, you have the option to end the conversation at that point if you wish.

3. Online Dating Downsides

Seeking a partner on dating apps can sometimes lead to a frustrating experience, influenced by a variety of factors that may or may not be within your control. Below, we'll explore common elements that can contribute to a less-than-ideal experience with dating apps:

#1. Swipe-Induced Insecurities

Let's get real for a moment. Dating apps have a way of chipping away at your confidence. In this digital realm, where decisions often hinge on a single swipe, a lackluster match or two can send you into a spiral of self-doubt. You might even start believing that unless you resemble a Hollywood heartthrob, you're destined for romantic doom. But let's pump the brakes on that negative thinking, shall we?

The truth is, those ladies perusing your profile are essentially judging a book by its cover. They don't really know you or have any inkling about your amazing personality. The same goes for you – it's all too easy to pass up someone based on a single snapshot. I mean, who has time to ponder, "Maybe this girl looks better in real life than in pictures?" Nobody. So, a quick left swipe it is.

On dating apps, we're all merchandise neatly arranged on a digital shelf, competing for attention like products in a supermarket. The catch? It's not just about what's inside; it's about how captivating your packaging appears. Here's the silver lining: you can jazz up that packaging and stand out from the crowd.

Let me share a little anecdote. Once, I stumbled upon a profile picture of a girl doing the infamous duck face. Now, I'm not particularly fond of the duck face, so I didn't bother exploring the rest of her photo gallery. A few days later, though, I encountered a picture of the same girl dancing on a table at some wild party. This time, I was intrigued. Funny thing is, as I perused her photos further, I came across the duck face picture once again. It was like discovering two entirely different personas within the same profile. Thank goodness she made that dancing pic her main attraction!

The lesson here? Profile pictures are your ticket to making an unforgettable first impression. It's not about how you look in everyday life; it's about how you appear in that snapshot. Those who thrive in the real world might have profile pictures that resemble the FBI's most-wanted shots or convey the look of someone who just lost a game of Poker. So, take your time and snap some attention-grabbing pics that'll leave her yearning to know more about the intriguing person behind them.

#2. There is no Perfect Icebreaker

Let's face it, There's no one-size-fits-all icebreaker. What cracks the ice for one might not for another. If she doesn't bite, don't try to make her chew. Respect her space and move on. Remember, persistence can be off-putting, so focus your energy where it's appreciated.

#3. Her Interest Can Wane

If you see the conversation spiraling away from its promising start or she's ghosting you, resist the urge to unleash a verbal tempest. Remember, women have their own unique tastes, and if something about you doesn't quite click with her, don't go looking for a magical fix. Not every chat that starts on a high note transforms into a date or a love story. Sometimes, the sparks fade, and that's okay.

#4. Grammar Mistakes Can Be a Turn-off

Now, I'm no grammar Nazi, but here's the scoop: if she knows her grammar, she won't tolerate egregious errors. We're not talking about Oxford comma here; it's about getting the basics right. Proper grammar is more than just punctuation and syntax; it reflects attention to detail and clear communication skills. Women often appreciate proper grammar because it signals respect for their intelligence and a commitment to effective conversation. In essence, it shows that you value the finer points of communication, making a positive impression that goes beyond words.

#5. Fierce Competition

- ❑ **You're Not the Only One She's Talking To:** Let's face it, the dating app arena is packed to the brim with contenders. Her inbox is buzzing with messages, so you're not the only one vying for her attention. The quest for exclusivity is admirable but remember, it's not handed out like candy. To have her undivided digital attention, you've got to earn it. Your conversation needs to be more captivating than a cat video. That's where playful exchanges come into play – they're not just about good vibes; they're the glue that binds connections. If she's enjoying the banter, she'll be itching to dive deeper into your world.

❑ **Your Profile Might Not Be Displayed:** Your profile might be playing hide-and-seek on her "Discovery" page, that magical place where profiles appear, ready for judgment day – the right swipe, left swipe, or the full-profile examination. Now, due to the sea of male users, your profile might not get the spotlight it deserves as she browses through the sea of faces.

❑ **She's Already Found What She's Looking For:** She might already be deep in conversation with other gentlemen and isn't exactly eager to dive into a new chat or scout for fresh matches.

Advice: Don't let bad experiences get you down. If it doesn't click the first time, shuffle and deal again! But here's a pro tip: Don't place all your dating hopes on the digital world. Always keep an eye out for opportunities to meet people in offline settings. Remember, love doesn't just live in the digital realm; it's out there in the real world too.

FINAL THOUGHTS

In this comprehensive guide, I've endeavored to equip you with a wide array of insights and strategies to navigate the intricate world of dating and seduction. Whether you're a shy teenager taking your first steps into the world of romance, someone recovering from a long-term relationship or divorce and feeling a bit rusty, or simply seeking to elevate your dating game, you'll find valuable information within these pages to enhance your interactions with women and ultimately shape the kind of relationships you desire.

I recognize that some of the concepts presented here may challenge preconceived notions you hold about dating and seduction. It's perfectly natural to feel a sense of reluctance when contemplating new approaches to interactions with women. However, it's essential to understand that playing it safe in the realm of seduction seldom leads to success. Avoiding risks can mean missing out on unique opportunities that may never come your way again. Trust in yourself and your capacity to make the best choices for your personal journey towards success in your romantic pursuits.

Remember the list you were encouraged to create at the beginning of this book? Knowing yourself and understanding your desires is a pivotal step towards finding the right partner. Before diving headfirst into the dating arena, take a moment to reflect on your intentions. Are you seeking a committed, long-term relationship, or are you open to more casual connections? Keeping your intentions at the forefront of your mind as you embark on this journey can help you avoid wasting time on individuals whose dating goals don't align with your own while opening doors to those who share your aspirations.

While it's essential to have clarity about your desires, it's equally important to remain open to the idea that what you want may manifest differently than you initially envisioned. Embrace the unexpected and relish every experience, whether they're delightful or challenging. Remember that every encounter has the potential to be a valuable lesson on your path to personal growth and romantic success.

In closing, think of your dating journey as a thrilling adventure filled with unexpected plot twists, humorous anecdotes, and heart-warming connections. Savor the sweet moments, and chuckle at the absurd ones. Remember, no matter how meticulously you plan your seduction strategies, life has a way of surprising us. So, go forth with newfound knowledge, armed with humor and an open heart. Your quest for love and meaningful connections is bound to be a story worth telling – one that might even earn you a bestseller!

Milton Keynes UK
Ingram Content Group UK Ltd.
UKHW020619291123
433416UK00016B/1230

9 798223 453727